On the Occasion of

From

Date

BIBLE
SECRETS
for
SUCCESSFUL
LIVING

G. E. Dean

BARBOUR
PUBLISHING, INC.
Uhrichsville, Ohio

Published by   Barbour Publishing, Inc.
               P.O. Box 719
               Uhrichsville, Ohio 44683
               http://www.barbourbooks.com

 Member of the
Evangelical Christian
Publishers Association

Printed in the United States of America.

Table of Contents

Blessings

And Moses said unto the LORD, O my Lord, I am not eloquent, neither heretofore, nor since thou hast spoken unto thy servant: but I am slow of speech, and of a slow tongue. Exodus 4:10

If we are not careful excuses to God will cause us to miss many blessings. God would not command us to do something that could not be done. Have faith and obey the Lord.

Thus saith the LORD, Let not the wise man glory in his wisdom, neither let the mighty man glory in his might, let not the rich man glory in his riches: But let him that glorieth glory in this, that he understandeth and knoweth me, that I am the LORD which exercise lovingkindness, judgment, and righteousness, in the earth: for in these things I delight, saith the LORD. Jeremiah 9:23-24

The greatest blessing of life is to know the Lord who gave it to us. Real meaning in life comes by trusting Him.

Every good gift and every perfect gift is from above, and cometh down from the Father of lights, with whom is no variableness, neither shadow of turning.
James 1:17

Remember that good comes from God. He will bless us if we just learn to trust and obey Him.

And whosoever doth not bear his cross, and come after me, cannot be my disciple. Luke 14:27

There is a cost involved in following Jesus. However, the cost cannot compare to the blessing of knowing Him.

Many are the afflictions of the righteous: but the LORD delivereth him out of them all. Psalm 34:19

God is faithful to care for those who belong to Him. It is a blessing to serve the Lord.

But the fruit of the Spirit is love, joy, peace, longsuffering, gentleness, goodness, faith, Meekness, temperance: against such there is no law.
Galatians 5:22-23

Being filled with the Holy Spirit will not only bless us but it will also be a blessing to those around us.

Happy is the man that feareth alway: but he that hardeneth his heart shall fall into mischief.
Proverbs 28:14

Blessings come to those who respect the Lord. Mischief comes to those who harden their hearts to God. The choice is ours to make.

It is good for me that I have been afflicted; that I might learn thy statutes. Psalm 119:71

Yes, blessings can come out of our difficulties. Tough times help us to lean more on the Lord.

But Simon's wife's mother lay sick of a fever, and anon they tell him of her. And he came and took her by the hand, and lifted her up; and immediately the fever left her, and she ministered unto them.
Mark 1:30-31

Once we have experienced the grace of God we should look to serve the Lord and others. Let your life be a channel of blessing.

Because thou servedst not the LORD thy God with joyfulness, and with gladness of heart, for the abundance of all things; Deuteronomy 28:47

Don't take for granted the blessings of the Lord and, most of all, don't forget the One who gave them to you.

And the LORD said unto Moses, How long will this people provoke me? and how long will it be ere they

believe me, for all the signs which I have shewed
among them? Numbers 14:11

How much more does God have to show us to prove
that He really loves us? Count your many blessings
and thank God for them. Serve the Lord with gladness.

And this they did, not as we hoped, but first gave
their own selves to the Lord, and unto us by the
will of God. 2 Corinthians 8:5

Giving ourselves completely to God and others is the
greatest gift we can ever give. By the way, this will be
the greatest blessings of our lives too.

And whatsoever ye do in word or deed, do all in the
name of the Lord Jesus, giving thanks to God and
the Father by him. Colossians 3:17

This is a great motto for living. Please the Lord and
see how doing that blesses your own life.

*And grieve not the holy Spirit of God, whereby ye
are sealed unto the day of redemption.*
Ephesians 4:30

Don't block the moving of God in your life. Let Him
be Lord of all. You can't afford to miss His blessings.

*So likewise, whosoever he be of you that forsaketh
not all that he hath, he cannot be my disciple.*
Luke 14:33

There is a price to be paid for being a follower of
Jesus. However, the blessings of God far outweigh
what the world can offer.

*But his delight is in the law of the LORD; and in his
law doth he meditate day and night. And he shall be
like a tree planted by the rivers of water, that
bringeth forth his fruit in his season; his leaf also
shall not wither; and whatsoever he doeth shall
prosper. Psalm 1:2-3*

True fulfillment and success come by finding the will
of God and doing it. Meditate on His Word and experience His blessings.

Blessed be the God and Father of our Lord Jesus Christ, who hath blessed us with all spiritual blessings in heavenly places in Christ: Ephesians 1:3

God is so good to us! Take time to count your blessings and you will find that things are not as bad as you thought.

Blessed is the man that walketh not in the counsel of the ungodly, nor standeth in the way of sinners, nor sitteth in the seat of the scornful. Psalm 1:1

The company we keep has a lot to do with our conduct. Surround yourself with those who love the Lord. You'll be blessed if you do.

Did not Achan the son of Zerah commit a trespass in the accursed thing, and wrath fell on all the congregation of Israel? and that man perished not alone in his iniquity. Joshua 22:20

None of us lives in isolation. What good we do blesses others and what evil we do hurts others. Be a blessing to yourself, others and to God.

*For they have sown the wind, and they shall reap
the whirlwind: it hath no stalk: the bud shall yield
no meal: if so be it yield, the strangers shall
swallow it up. Hosea 8:7*

People and nations suffer for sowing sin. Live a holy
life by God's power and experience the blessings of
God instead of the consequences of sin.

*Blessed are the merciful: for they shall obtain mercy.
Matthew 5:7*

It's amazing how our actions will come back to haunt
or bless us. Be a person that possesses both moral
excellence and mercy. God will make you a blessing
if you do.

*As we have therefore opportunity, let us do good
unto all men, especially unto them who are of the
household of faith. Galatians 6:10*

Don't see how little you can do for God and others.
Give your best to others. Be more concerned about
being a blessing rather than receiving a blessing.

And whatsoever ye do, do it heartily, as to the Lord, and not unto men; Colossians 3:23

The person we need to seek to please is the Lord Jesus. When we do we will be a blessing to others. Give your best today for the glory of God.

And there are also many other things which Jesus did, the which, if they should be written every one, I suppose that even the world itself could not contain the books that should be written. Amen. John 21:25

We serve a great Lord. Have you taken time to count His blessings upon your life? Thank you, Jesus, for being so good to us.

Then said the LORD, Doest thou well to be angry? Jonah 4:4

What a good question. Stop thinking about what is wrong and think on the good. Anger destroys. Count your many blessings.

The LORD is good unto them that wait for him, to the soul that seeketh him. Lamentations 3:25

God longs to pour out His blessings upon us. Wait on Him and seek Him and watch the windows of Heaven open for you.

And said, If thou wilt diligently hearken to the voice of the LORD thy God, and wilt do that which is right in his sight, and wilt give ear to his commandments, and keep all his statutes, I will put none of these diseases upon thee, which I have brought upon the Egyptians: for I am the LORD that healeth thee. Exodus 15:26

He is still the same wonderful Lord. Let Him bring healing to your mind, soul and body. He is Lord. Seek Him and experience His blessings.

For the LORD God is a sun and shield: the LORD will give grace and glory: no good thing will he withhold from them that walk uprightly. Psalm 84:11

The Lord longs to bless your life. Walk uprightly and see Him work in your circumstances.

*For they loved the praise of men more than the
praise of God. John 12:43*

We are probably far more concerned with what people
think rather than what God thinks. That's a mistake.
Live a life that pleases God and you will be a blessing
to others.

*Honour the LORD with thy substance, and with the
firstfruits of all thine increase: So shall thy barns
be filled with plenty, and thy presses shall burst
out with new wine. Proverbs 3:9-10*

When we honor the Lord with our possessions, He
honors us with His blessing. "Serve the Lord with
gladness." He loves you!

*And all these blessings shall come on thee, and
overtake thee, if thou shalt hearken unto the voice of
the LORD thy God. Deuteronomy 28:2*

Obeying the Lord definitely has its benefits. Let God's
blessings "Come on thee, and overtake thee." Obey
the Lord.

Blessed be the Lord, who daily loadeth us with benefits, even the God of our salvation. Selah.
Psalm 68:19

Take time to count your blessings. You too will agree that God has loaded us with blessings.

Only take heed to thyself, and keep thy soul diligently, lest thou forget the things which thine eyes have seen, and lest they depart from thy heart all the days of thy life: but teach them thy sons, and thy sons' sons; Deuteronomy 4:9

Constantly remember God's blessings. To forget them is to rob ourselves and our children of a great blessing.

Blessed is every one that feareth the LORD; that walketh in his ways. For thou shalt eat the labour of thine hands: happy shalt thou be, and it shall be well with thee. Psalm 128:1-2

Respect and fear of the Lord leads to wonderful blessings. He knows what is best for you and me. Let's follow Him.

And Jethro rejoiced for all the goodness which the LORD had done to Israel, whom he had delivered out of the hand of the Egyptians. Exodus 18:9

The happiest people in the world are those that recognize God's blessings. Take time to count your blessings.

If ye then, being evil, know how to give good gifts unto your children, how much more shall your Father which is in heaven give good things to them that ask him? Matthew 7:11

God is so good. He longs to bless your life. Follow His ways and experience His blessings.

All that the Father giveth me shall come to me; and him that cometh to me I will in no wise cast out. John 6:37

Jesus loves you! Have you experienced His love? Come to Him and experience His blessings.

And now abideth faith, hope, charity, these three; but the greatest of these is charity. 1 Corinthians 13:13

Being a recipient and channel of God's love is the greatest blessing of life. Accept God's love for you and pass it on to others.

Delight thyself also in the LORD; and he shall give thee the desires of thine heart. Psalm 37:4

Let the Lord be the delight of your life and life will truly be a blessing. Take God at His Word.

And forgat his works, and his wonders that he had shewed them. Psalm 78:11

Don't forget God's blessings. If you do you will rob yourself of life's greatest memories.

The liberal soul shall be made fat: and he that watereth shall be watered also himself.
Proverbs 11:25

The way to genuine prosperity is paved with giving to God and others. We are blessed most when we learn to be a blessing.

LORD, make me to know mine end, and the measure of my days, what it is; that I may know how frail I am. Behold, thou hast made my days as an handbreadth; and mine age is as nothing before thee: verily every man at his best state is altogether vanity. Selah. Psalm 39:4-5

Life is fragile. Every day is a blessing from God.

Hearken unto thy father that begat thee, and despise not thy mother when she is old. Proverbs 23:22

Respect for parents is not only a blessing to both child and parents but is also a cornerstone for a righteous society.

The LORD hath done great things for us; whereof we are glad. Psalm 126:3

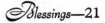

Count your many blessings. God is so good to us.

*My son, despise not the chastening of the LORD;
neither be weary of his correction: For whom the
LORD loveth he correcteth; even as a father the son
in whom he delighteth. Proverbs 3:11-12*

God's discipline is an act of love. In time you'll see
the blessing of that loving discipline.

*Turn thou us unto thee, O LORD, and we shall be
turned; renew our days as of old.
Lamentations 5:21*

Have you been a drop-out for the Lord? There is hope.
Turn to Him. Let Him bring the blessings to your life
like the old days. He can do it.

*When thou hast eaten and art full, then thou shalt
bless the LORD thy God for the good land which he
hath given thee. Beware that thou forget not the
LORD thy God, in not keeping his commandments,*

and his judgments, and his statutes, which I
command thee this day: Deuteronomy 8:10-11

In the midst of all your blessings, don't forget the One
who blessed you.

And which of you with taking thought can add to his
stature one cubit? Luke 12:25

Worry is waste of time. Faith in God is a blessing that
cannot be measured. Which one will you choose?

Be still, and know that I am God: I will be exalted
among the heathen, I will be exalted in the earth.
Psalm 46:10

God is working all around you. Take time to see what
He is doing and you'll be blessed.

Every man shall give as he is able, according to the
blessing of the LORD thy God which he hath given
thee. Deuteronomy 16:17

Do you just receive from God? The Bible says that we should gladly give back to God.

Honour the LORD with thy substance, and with the firstfruits of all thine increase: So shall thy barns be filled with plenty, and thy presses shall burst out with new wine. Proverbs 3:9-10

God's blessings come to our lives when we honor Him with our possessions. You can't outgive God.

Bring ye all the tithes into the storehouse, that there may be meat in mine house, and prove me now herewith, saith the LORD of hosts, if I will not open you the windows of heaven, and pour you out a blessing, that there shall not be room enough to receive it. Malachi 3:10

God blesses the faithful who give back to Him. Try tithing and see God's blessing in your life.

Charity

*And he touched her hand, and the fever left her: and
she arose, and ministered unto them. Matthew 8:15*

It is perfectly natural for a person who has been transformed by the power of God to serve Him and others.
Christian, what have you done for the cause of Christ
since you have met Him?

*Let this mind be in you, which was also in Christ
Jesus: Who, being in the form of God, thought it not
robbery to be equal with God: But made himself of
no reputation, and took upon him the form of a
servant, and was made in the likeness of men.
Philippians 2:5-7*

We will not really become happy until we learn to
serve God and others. Put on the mind of Christ.

But ye, brethren, be not weary in well doing.
2 Thessalonians 3:13

Keep on doing good whether others appreciate it or not. God is keeping the records that count.

If he hath wronged thee, or oweth thee ought, put that on mine account. Philemon 1:18

Is there someone in need that you could help? Ask God to help you see and meet the needs of others.

And David said, Is there yet any that is left of the house of Saul, that I may shew him kindness for Jonathan's sake? 2 Samuel 9:1

Are we looking to do acts of kindness for others or are we just waiting for others to do for us? Think it over.

And above all things have fervent charity among yourselves: for charity shall cover the multitude of sins. 1 Peter 4:8

Sincere love has profound effects. Love the Lord and others and watch God work.

And Jesus, moved with compassion, put forth his hand, and touched him, and saith unto him, I will; be thou clean. And as soon as he had spoken, immediately the leprosy departed from him, and he was cleansed. Mark 1:41-42

The question is this: Will we too reach out to the hurting and lonely and let them know that we care? There may be more healing in our touch and concern than we ever realize.

And some of the chief of the fathers, when they came to the house of the LORD which is at Jerusalem, offered freely for the house of God to set it up in his place: Ezra 2:68

Joyful giving is a characteristic of those who love the Lord. Are you giving with a grateful heart?

And he came to Capernaum: and being in the house he asked them, What was it that ye disputed among yourselves by the way? But they held their peace: for by the way they had disputed among themselves, who should be the greatest. Mark 9:33-34

Are we as guilty as the disciples in wanting others to serve us instead of us serving others? Remember, Jesus is our example. To be great for God you must be a servant.

But a certain Samaritan, as he journeyed, came where he was: and when he saw him, he had compassion on him. Luke 10:33

Is your heart tough or tender? Can you still feel compassion for those in need? Many people are hurting. Be a good Samaritan for someone today.

And he saw also a certain poor widow casting in thither two mites. And he said, Of a truth I say unto you, that this poor widow hath cast in more than they all: For all these have of their abundance cast in unto the offerings of God: but she of her penury hath cast in all the living that she had. Luke 21:2-4

Do we really know the meaning of sacrifice? When we think we have given our all, let's remember the poor widow.

For even the Son of man came not to be ministered unto, but to minister, and to give his life a ransom for many. Mark 10:45

Caring for others not only allows us to follow Jesus' example but it also blesses those we serve and ourselves. Let's all be God's ministers in Jesus' name and for Jesus' sake.

But when he saw the multitudes, he was moved with compassion on them, because they fainted, and were scattered abroad, as sheep having no shepherd. Then saith he unto his disciples, The harvest truly is plenteous, but the labourers are few; Pray ye therefore the Lord of the harvest, that he will send forth labourers into his harvest. Matthew 9:36-38

Jesus has a heart for all people. Let's be one of His workers in the harvest of hurting humanity.

And let our's also learn to maintain good works for
necessary uses, that they be not unfruitful.
Titus 3:14

Christians should be useful and productive citizens.
Honor the Lord by doing good works.

Every man according as he purposeth in his heart,
so let him give; not grudgingly, or of necessity: for
God loveth a cheerful giver. 2 Corinthians 9:7

Our world needs more cheerful givers. Will you be
one?

Blessed is he that considereth the poor: the LORD
will deliver him in time of trouble. Psalm 41:1

Seek to bless others who can't help themselves and
God will take care of you.

Let all your things be done with charity.
1 Corinthians 16:14

Every activity done and every life touched by you should be filled with love from above. What a great witness for our Lord!

And the Lord said unto Cain, Where is Abel thy brother? And he said, I know not: Am I my brother's keeper? Genesis 4:9

We can not avoid the fact that we are to be concerned about one another. Let's take our head out of the sand and help a person in need. We are our brother's keeper!

I must work the works of him that sent me, while it is day: the night cometh, when no man can work. John 9:4

Time is a precious gift. Make the most of it. Serve the Lord and others with all you've got.

Bear ye one another's burdens, and so fulfil the law of Christ. Galatians 6:2

There's always someone who has more problems than yourself. Take time today to help a friend in need. This is the kind of life that pleases the Lord.

Let no man seek his own, but every man another's wealth. 1 Corinthians 10:24

Are we so wrapped up in our lives that we forget there are those in much deeper need? Seek to help someone in need.

I have shewed you all things, how that so labouring ye ought to support the weak, and to remember the words of the Lord Jesus, how he said, It is more blessed to give than to receive. Acts 20:35

Have you made the wonderful discovery of giving? If not, give it a try. Receiving is a blessing, but you'll find giving to be even better.

And the King shall answer and say unto them, Verily I say unto you, Inasmuch as ye have done it unto one

*of the least of these my brethren, ye have done it
unto me. Matthew 25:40*

When we help people in need, we are helping the Lord. Let God make you a blessing to someone else today.

*Let brotherly love continue. Be not forgetful to
entertain strangers: for thereby some have
entertained angels unawares. Hebrews 13:1-2*

Be loving. Be helpful. You never know who you may be helping.

*Whoso stoppeth his ears at the cry of the poor, he
also shall cry himself, but shall not be heard.
Proverbs 21:13*

Refusing to help those in need does have its consequences. Have a heart to help others and God will see that there will be those who help you in your time of need.

And whosoever of you will be the chiefest, shall be servant of all. Mark 10:44

Greatness in God's eyes is determined by our service to others. We may not be as great as we supposed. Learn to serve others.

Pure religion and undefiled before God and the Father is this, To visit the fatherless and widows in their affliction, and to keep himself unspotted from the world. James 1:27

Pure religion is known by its action. Minister to others in the name of Jesus. This will bless God, others and yourself.

Let him that stole steal no more: but rather let him labour, working with his hands the thing which is good, that he may have to give to him that needeth. Ephesians 4:28

It is good for a person to work. However, don't forget that we are to share the fruits of our labors with those who are in genuine need. Is there someone you should help today?

But if any provide not for his own, and specially for those of his own house, he hath denied the faith, and is worse than an infidel. 1 Timothy 5:8

Whatever happened to families taking care of their own? We all have a responsibility to do our best to provide for those in our families that cannot take care of themselves.

And whosoever will be chief among you, let him be your servant: Matthew 20:27

Greatness in God's eyes is measured by the willing spirit of servanthood. See to the needs of others and God will take care of you.

Ye have lived in pleasure on the earth, and been wanton; ye have nourished your hearts, as in a day of slaughter. James 5:5

Are we guilty of abusing the blessings of God? Let's share the things God has given us. It's the right thing to do.

Moreover it is required in stewards, that a man be found faithful. 1 Corinthians 4:2

What have you done with what God has given you? Have you been a good steward? Use your possessions, your talents, and your life to bless God and others.

But I fear, lest by any means, as the serpent beguiled Eve through his subtilty, so your minds should be corrupted from the simplicity that is in Christ. 2 Corinthians 11:3

Make sure that your philosphy of life is built upon the Word of God. Know what you believe and live what you believe.

And Jehoshaphat said unto the king of Israel, Enquire, I pray thee, at the word of the LORD to day. 1 Kings 22:5

Ask the Lord for wisdom before you make that decision. He knows what is best for you.

Honour the L<small>ORD</small> with thy substance, and with the firstfruits of all thine increase: So shall thy barns be filled with plenty, and thy presses shall burst out with new wine. Proverbs 3:9-10

Honor the Lord with your possessions and He will take care of you.

And all the wise men, that wrought all the work of the sanctuary, came every man from his work which they made; And they spake unto Moses, saying, The people bring much more than enough for the service of the work, which the L<small>ORD</small> commanded to make. Exodus 36:4-5

Oh that God's people would have this same kind of generosity today. We should gladly give to the Lord because He has given so much to us.

A good man out of the good treasure of his heart bringeth forth that which is good; and an evil man out of the evil treasure of his heart bringeth forth that which is evil: for of the abundance of the heart his mouth speaketh. Luke 6:45

Our words tell us a lot about our hearts. Fill your heart with the love and wisdom of God. Your words will show that you love Him.

And all the princes and all the people rejoiced, and brought in, and cast into the chest, until they had made an end. 2 Chronicles 24:10

God loves cheerful givers. Are you giving as you should? Are you giving with the right attitude?

Upon the first day of the week let every one of you lay by him in store, as God hath prospered him, that there be no gatherings when I come.
1 Corinthians 16:2

This is one of the Biblical models of stewardship. Let's give back to God because He has given so much to us.

And, behold, there are last which shall be first, and there are first which shall be last. Luke 13:30

It is obvious that God has a different definition of success than the philosophy of this world. Servanthood is big in God's eyes.

Let all your things be done with charity.
1 Corinthians 16:14

The motivation for life should be love for the Lord and love for others. "Do all things in love."

But he that is greatest among you shall be your
servant. Matthew 23:11

Do you really want to be great? Be a servant. Be a great person today.

Take heed to yourselves, that your heart be not
deceived, and ye turn aside, and serve other gods,
and worship them; Deuteronomy 11:16

Is that material object or pleasure becoming your god? Be careful. Seek the Lord with all your heart.

Bring ye all the tithes into the storehouse, that there may be meat in mine house, and prove me now herewith, saith the LORD of hosts, if I will not open you the windows of heaven, and pour you out a blessing, that there shall not be room enough to receive it. Malachi 3:10

Give to the Lord and He will bless you. You can't out-give God.

For, brethren, ye have been called unto liberty; only use not liberty for an occasion to the flesh, but by love serve one another. Galatians 5:13

Jesus sets us free not to serve our selfish interests but rather to serve others. Help someone in Jesus' name today.

Our fathers have sinned, and are not; and we have borne their iniquities. Lamentations 5:7

Before you make that foolish decision or decide to cast your life to the wind, think about who might have to bear the consequences of that sin. Think about those you love. Make the right decision.

Counsel

But above all things, my brethren, swear not, neither by heaven, neither by the earth, neither by any other oath: but let your yea be yea; and your nay, nay; lest ye fall into condemnation. James 5:12

There is no need for an honest man to swear. A simple yes or no will do.

Providing for honest things, not only in the sight of the Lord, but also in the sight of men.
2 Corinthians 8:21

The Christian should always seek to do what is right before God and man. Honesty is a wonderful witness for Jesus.

Neither give place to the devil. Ephesians 4:27

Compromise is the beginning of great heartache. Stand up for God and resist the devil.

A friend loveth at all times, and a brother is born for adversity. Proverbs 17:17

Good friends are hard to find. Let's seek to be the good friends God want us to be.

Thou shalt not go up and down as a talebearer among thy people: neither shalt thou stand against the blood of thy neighbour: I am the LORD. Leviticus 19:16

Slandering others can heap untold heartache on others and yourself. Be kind and gentle with the reputations of others.

As the fining pot for silver, and the furnace for gold; so is a man to his praise. Proverbs 27:21

How we handle praise is just as important as how we handle criticism. Let all of your circumstances and how you handle them be a testimony for the glory of God.

Abstain from all appearance of evil.
1 Thessalonians 5:22

We could save ourselves a lot of grief if we would just heed this advice. Avoid even the appearance of evil.

Keep thy heart with all diligence; for out of it are
the issues of life. Proverbs 4:23

Let's be careful what we allow to enter our hearts. Our eyes and ears need to be turned to the things of God.

Only let your conversation be as it becometh the
gospel of Christ: that whether I come and see you,
or else be absent, I may hear of your affairs, that ye
stand fast in one spirit, with one mind striving
together for the faith of the gospel; Philippians 1:27

Christian, is your lifestyle one that is a good testimony for Jesus? Don't compromise. Stand up for Jesus every day.

He that keepeth his mouth keepeth his life: but he that openeth wide his lips shall have destruction.
Proverbs 13:3

What this world needs is not more speakers but more listeners. Learn to measure your words carefully.

But woe unto you, Pharisees! for ye tithe mint and rue and all manner of herbs, and pass over judgment and the love of God: these ought ye to have done, and not to leave the other undone. Luke 11:42

Godly activities without love are empty. Godly service with love is blessed and beautiful. Serve the Lord with a heart of love.

Be not rash with thy mouth, and let not thine heart be hasty to utter any thing before God: for God is in

heaven, and thou upon earth: therefore let thy words be few. Ecclesiastes 5:2

We must measure our words before the Lord. Next time let's think before we speak. God is listening.

Lest haply, after he hath laid the foundation, and is not able to finish it, all that behold it begin to mock him, Saying, This man began to build, and was not able to finish. Luke 14:29-30

The conclusion of a project is as important as the beginning. Complete the task that lies before you.

And I looked, and rose up, and said unto the nobles, and to the rulers, and to the rest of the people, Be not ye afraid of them: remember the Lord, which is great and terrible, and fight for your brethren, your sons, and your daughters, your wives, and your houses. Nehemiah 4:14

"Remember the Lord." What great advice. Don't be afraid of what you face. Remember the Lord. He is the Prince of Peace.

His mother saith unto the servants, Whatsoever he saith unto you, do it. John 2:5

This is still good advice for today. Do whatever Jesus tells you to do.

A prudent man foreseeth the evil, and hideth himself: but the simple pass on, and are punished.
Proverbs 22:3

Are you prudent or simple? Claim the promise of James 1:5, "If any of you lack wisdom, let him ask of God, that giveth to all men liberally, and upbraideth not; and it shall be given him," and you will save yourself a lot of grief.

While he yet spake, behold, a bright cloud overshadowed them: and behold a voice out of the cloud, which said, This is my beloved Son, in whom I am well pleased; hear ye him. Matthew 17:5

This is good advice for today and every day. Take time to study the life of Jesus and see what He has to say to you.

Thou shalt rise up before the hoary head, and honour the face of the old man, and fear thy God: I am the LORD. Leviticus 19:32

We need old-fashioned respect for the elderly. When we don't have it, all of society loses.

And there came a voice out of the cloud, saying, This is my beloved Son: hear him. Luke 9:35

This is great advice. Listen to what Jesus has to say. He has the best plan for your life.

He that loveth silver shall not be satisfied with silver; nor he that loveth abundance with increase: this is also vanity. Ecclesiastes 5:10

The greedy person will never be satisfied no matter how much he has.

Reprove not a scorner, lest he hate thee: rebuke a wise man, and he will love thee. Proverbs 9:8

Are you glad or mad when someone tries to give advice? Our response tells much about our character.

Little children, keep yourselves from idols. Amen.
1 John 5:21

Idolatry comes in all forms to tempt all people, even God's people. Christian, keep your eyes on Jesus.

Put on the whole armour of God, that ye may be able to stand against the wiles of the devil.
Ephesians 6:11

When getting ready for the day, don't forget to put on the whole armor of God.

But Jonah rose up to flee unto Tarshish from the presence of the LORD, and went down to Joppa; and he found a ship going to Tarshish: so he paid the fare thereof, and went down into it, to go with them unto Tarshish from the presence of the LORD.
Jonah 1:3

Are you running from the Lord? Jonah found out the hard way that running from God doesn't pay. Let's learn a lesson from Jonah.

Go from the presence of a foolish man, when thou perceivest not in him the lips of knowledge.
Proverbs 14:7

Stay away from foolish people. Surround yourself with those who love the Lord.

He, that being often reproved hardeneth his neck, shall suddenly be destroyed, and that without remedy. Proverbs 29:1

Take heed to the rebuke of the Lord. He does it for your own good. If you don't, the consequences are terrible.

He made a pit, and digged it, and is fallen into the ditch which he made. Psalm 7:15

The troublemaker makes only real trouble for himself.

*Lay not up for yourselves treasures upon earth,
where moth and rust doth corrupt, and where thieves
break through and steal: But lay up for yourselves
treasures in heaven, where neither moth nor rust
doth corrupt, and where thieves do not break
through nor steal: Matthew 6:19-20*

The things of this world don't last. Heavenly treasures
last forever. Be a wise investor.

*Woe unto them that are wise in their own eyes, and
prudent in their own sight! Isaiah 5:21*

This should take care of any over confidence we have.
We need the wisdom of the Lord to make the right
decision. Have you prayed about your next decision?

*But they refused to hearken, and pulled away the
shoulder, and stopped their ears, that they should not
hear. Yea, they made their hearts as an adamant*

stone, lest they should hear the law, and the words which the LORD of hosts hath sent in his spirit by the former prophets: therefore came a great wrath from the LORD of hosts. Zechariah 7:11-12

Are you one of those people that just want to hear that which is convenient? Hear the whole counsel of God and believe. This is the fulfilled life.

For the love of money is the root of all evil: which while some coveted after, they have erred from the faith, and pierced themselves through with many sorrows. 1 Timothy 6:10

Remember, we are to love people and use things, not love things and use people. Don't allow greed to consume your heart.

But I say unto you, That every idle word that men shall speak, they shall give account thereof in the day of judgment. Matthew 12:36

Words can have a tremendous impact. What kind of impact do your words make?

Not that which goeth into the mouth defileth a man;
but that which cometh out of the mouth, this
defileth a man. Matthew 15:11

Jesus said that we should be more concerned with what comes out of our mouths than what we put in our mouths. What's been coming out of your mouth?

For the LORD, the God of Israel, saith that he hateth
putting away: for one covereth violence with his
garment, saith the LORD of hosts: therefore take heed
to your spirit, that ye deal not treacherously.
Malachi 2:16

The Lord hates divorce because He knows the heartache it brings. Let the Lord be the foundation of your marriage. He can preserve it.

Whoso keepeth his mouth and his tongue keepeth his
soul from troubles. Proverbs 21:23

The little song for children says, "Oh be careful little mouth what you say." It's great advice for big people too.

*The words of a talebearer are as wounds, and they
go down into the innermost parts of the belly.
Proverbs 26:22*

Gossip wounds and is seldom forgotten. Be careful
what you say.

*And that ye study to be quiet, and to do your own
business, and to work with your own hands, as we
commanded you; That ye may walk honestly toward
them that are without, and that ye may have lack
of nothing. 1 Thessalonians 4:11-12*

If we are busy doing what we should, we will not have
time to judge others. In addition to this, we will have
the satisfaction of a job well done. Give your best at
work today.

*Wine is a mocker, strong drink is raging: and
whosoever is deceived thereby is not wise.
Proverbs 20:1*

Alcohol is still making fools out of people. Don't
become a slave to alcohol.

*Set a watch, O L*ORD*, before my mouth; keep the door of my lips. Psalm 141:3*

This is a prayer that could save all of us much heartache. Be careful what you say. Let the Lord be the master of your conversation.

*Honour thy father and thy mother: that thy days may be long upon the land which the L*ORD *thy God giveth thee. Exodus 20:12*

We must get back to the basics of God's commands. They're for our own good.

And I say unto you my friends, Be not afraid of them that kill the body, and after that have no more that they can do. But I will forewarn you whom ye shall fear: Fear him, which after he hath killed hath power to cast into hell; yea, I say unto you, Fear him. Luke 12:4-5

Dear friend, remember that you must not only love God but also reverence Him. He will determine the fate of your soul for eternity.

But Jeshurun waxed fat, and kicked: thou art waxen
fat, thou art grown thick, thou art covered with
fatness; then he forsook God which made him, and
lightly esteemed the Rock of his salvation.
Deuteronomy 32:15

Prosperity can be a curse if we let it take the place of God.

Draw nigh to God, and he will draw nigh to you.
Cleanse your hands, ye sinners; and purify your
hearts, ye double minded. Be afflicted, and mourn,
and weep: let your laughter be turned to mourning,
and your joy to heaviness. Humble yourselves in the
sight of the Lord, and he shall lift you up.
James 4:8-10

Heed these instructions and experience new life.

There is a way that seemeth right unto a man, but
the end thereof are the ways of death.
Proverbs 16:25

You can be sincerely wrong. Be sure that you follow God's way to eternal life. "Jesus saith unto him, I am the way, the truth, and the life: no man cometh unto the Father, but by me. (John 14:6)

Thou shalt not take the name of the LORD thy God in vain: for the LORD will not hold him guiltless that taketh his name in vain. Deuteronomy 5:11

Think twice before you utter the Lord's name in vain. You will be held accountable for your words.

But shun profane and vain babblings: for they will increase unto more ungodliness. 2 Timothy 2:16

Idle gossip will always lead to godlessness. Be careful in what you say and what you hear.

Obey them that have the rule over you, and submit yourselves: for they watch for your souls, as they that must give account, that they may do it with joy, and not with grief: for that is unprofitable for you. Hebrews 13:17

Show respect to those who instruct you in the ways of the Lord. They are not hired hands. They are called of God to proclaim His Word.

They soon forgat his works; they waited not for his counsel: Psalm 106:13

God's people hurt themselves when they do not remember Him when making decisions.

And they worshipped him, and returned to Jerusalem with great joy: Luke 24:52

Worshipping the Lord has many benefits. One of them is joy. Be sure to be involved in your church's worship service this Sunday.

So when they continued asking him, he lifted up himself, and said unto them, He that is without sin among you, let him first cast a stone at her. John 8:7

Don't be too quick to judge someone else. God judges all. We need to remember that all have sinned and come short of the glory of God. That includes us too.

He that walketh with wise men shall be wise: but a companion of fools shall be destroyed.
Proverbs 13:20

With whom we associate does make a difference. Are your friends wise or foolish?

He that is void of wisdom despiseth his neighbour: but a man of understanding holdeth his peace.
Proverbs 11:12

Are we void of wisdom or are we full of understanding?

Abram dwelled in the land of Canaan, and Lot dwelled in the cities of the plain, and pitched his tent toward Sodom. But the men of Sodom were wicked

and sinners before the LORD exceedingly.
Genesis 13:13

Be careful where you plant your life. It does make a difference.

$\mathscr{E}$ncouragement

*Fulfil ye my joy, that ye be likeminded, having the
same love, being of one accord, of one mind.*
Philippians 2:2

Unity in the fellowship of the church is priceless.
Have the heart and the mind of Christ and encourage
others to do likewise.

*Even the youths shall faint and be weary, and the
young men shall utterly fall: But they that wait upon
the LORD shall renew their strength; they shall mount
up with wings as eagles; they shall run, and not be
weary; and they shall walk, and not faint.*
Isaiah 40:30-31

The Lord can give you the strength and encouragement you need. Let go and let God have His way in
your heart.

And God said, Let there be light: and there was light. Genesis 1:3

Just as God brought light to brighten the universe, He can do the same for your soul in despair. Let Him bring the light of hope and encouragement to your life.

Then the people of the land weakened the hands of the people of Judah, and troubled them in building, Ezra 4:4

There will always be those who seek to discourage those who love the Lord. Keep your eyes on Him. If God is in it, no one can stop you.

And David was greatly distressed; for the people spake of stoning him, because the soul of all the people was grieved, every man for his sons and for his daughters: but David encouraged himself in the LORD his God. 1 Samuel 30:6

The Lord is bigger than the crisis you face. Find strength and encouragement in the Lord. He cares about you.

But ye, brethren, be not weary in well doing.
2 Thessalonians 3:13

Don't give up. Be faithful to the Lord. Be encouraged.
God will bless your efforts.

Judge not, that ye be not judged. Matthew 7:1

Jesus did not call us to be judgmental and critical. He
has called us to love one another. Be an encourager.
We need more of them.

And Ephraim their father mourned many days, and
his brethren came to comfort him. 1 Chronicles 7:22

Is there someone you know who has a heavy heart?
Take time to comfort and encourage them.

Being confident of this very thing, that he which hath
begun a good work in you will perform it until the
day of Jesus Christ: Philippians 1:6

The Lord always finishes what He begins. Don't be discouraged, Christian. God is still at work in your life.

Obey them that have the rule over you, and submit yourselves: for they watch for your souls, as they that must give account, that they may do it with joy, and not with grief: for that is unprofitable for you.
Hebrews 13:17

Respect and encourage those who have been given spiritual leadership responsibilities. Most of all, be sure to pray for them.

And Judas and Silas, being prophets also themselves, exhorted the brethren with many words, and confirmed them. Acts 15:32

This world is in dire need of encouragers. As Christians we have the most hope-inspiring message of all. Encourage a friend by telling them that Jesus cares.

Beloved, I wish above all things that thou mayest prosper and be in health, even as thy soul prospereth. 3 John 1:2

It should be our desire to wish the best for everyone. Take time to encourage a friend today.

And why beholdest thou the mote that is in thy brother's eye, but perceivest not the beam that is in thine own eye? Luke 6:41

The Lord never intended for us to keep score on others. We are to look to Him and make sure that our lives are what they should be. Then and only then can we be in a position to really encourage others.

Heaviness in the heart of man maketh it stoop: but a good word maketh it glad. Proverbs 12:25

We have no idea of the burdens that some people carry. Always be ready to speak a word of encouragement.

Jesus said unto him, If thou canst believe, all things are possible to him that believeth. Mark 9:23

There's enough doubt and discouragement in this world. What we need is faith in God. He's the One who can bring encouragement and joy to life. Believe in the Lord and let him change your life.

But I say unto you, That every idle word that men shall speak, they shall give account thereof in the day of judgment. Matthew 12:36

This truth should really help us measure our words. Let's don't be careless with our speech. Seek to honor the Lord and encourage others.

And Jonathan, Saul's son, arose, and went to David into the wood, and strengthened his hand in God. 1 Samuel 23:16

A child of God may need some encouragement from you today. It may be your pastor, Sunday School teacher, or next-door neighbor. Encourage them, as Jonathan went to David.

Therefore thou art inexcusable, O man, whosoever thou art that judgest: for wherein thou judgest another, thou condemnest thyself; for thou that judgest doest the same things. Romans 2:1

We are not called to be judges of other people. We are called to love them. Encourage someone today by caring about them.

Be of good courage, and he shall strengthen your heart, all ye that hope in the LORD. Psalm 31:24

Don't be discouraged. God is still on the throne. Place your hope in the Lord.

Let no corrupt communication proceed out of your mouth, but that which is good to the use of edifying, that it may minister grace unto the hearers. Ephesians 4:29

How are we communicating? Are we critical and negative toward others or do we seek to encourage others?

But shun profane and vain babblings: for they will increase unto more ungodliness. 2 Timothy 2:16

Idle gossip and nonsense can lead to serious problems. Make your words count. Be an encourager.

*Use hospitality one to another without grudging.
1 Peter 4:9*

Is there someone you know who needs good old-fashioned hospitality? Be a good neighbor. Your word of encouragement may be the medicine they need.

*But if any man love God, the same is known of him.
1 Corinthians 8:3*

Don't be discouraged, dear Christian. God knows you and loves you. Keep loving the Lord.

For consider him that endured such contradiction of sinners against himself, lest ye be wearied and faint in your minds. Hebrews 12:3

If you're discouraged and down don't forget what Jesus did for you. He is our example, our inspiration and our source of power. Lean on Him.

Not forsaking the assembling of ourselves together, as the manner of some is; but exhorting one another: and so much the more, as ye see the day approaching. Hebrews 10:25

Don't neglect worship attendance. It is important. We need the encouragement of other Christians as we walk with the Lord.

For I have told him that I will judge his house for ever for the iniquity which he knoweth; because his sons made themselves vile, and he restrained them not. 1 Samuel 3:13

Parents, are we doing all we can do to encourage our children to live for the Lord? We have an awesome responsibility. Let's give it our best.

But exhort one another daily, while it is called To day; lest any of you be hardened through the deceitfulness of sin. Hebrews 3:13

Everyone needs encouragement. Everyone needs it on a regular basis. Involve yourself in the ministry of encouragement.

Then the disciples, every man according to his ability, determined to send relief unto the brethren which dwelt in Judaea: Acts 11:29

This is real Christianity. Christians should be there to help and encourage each other.

And his heart was lifted up in the ways of the LORD: moreover he took away the high places and groves out of Judah. 2 Chronicles 17:6

Have you been down? Follow the ways of the Lord and be lifted up in spirit. God can replace your sadness with His joy.

Pleasant words are as an honeycomb, sweet to the soul, and health to the bones. Proverbs 16:24

We have had enough of cynicism and sarcasm. Let's speak words that "are pleasant as a honeycomb." Be an encourager.

I thank my God upon every remembrance of you. Philippians 1:3

A grateful heart is a happy heart. Don't let bitterness and resentment run your life. Be grateful for others and let them know that you appreciate them.

Whither shall we go up? our brethren have discouraged our heart, saying, The people is greater and taller than we; the cities are great and walled up to heaven; and moreover we have seen the sons of the Anakims there. Deuteronomy 1:28

Don't discourage others from following the Lord. Be an encourager.

I am Alpha and Omega, the beginning and the ending, saith the Lord, which is, and which was, and which is to come, the Almighty. Revelation 1:8

It's always encouraging to remember that God is still on the throne. You can depend on Him.

A soft answer turneth away wrath: but grievous words stir up anger. Proverbs 15:1

We need more soft answers in our world and less bitterness. Be an encourager. Be kind.

Train up a child in the way he should go: and when he is old, he will not depart from it. Proverbs 22:6

Don't be discouraged, dear Godly parents. Claim this verse for your wayward child.

And, ye fathers, provoke not your children to wrath: but bring them up in the nurture and admonition of the Lord. Ephesians 6:4

Dads play a key role in the self-esteem of a child. Dad, are you encouraging your child?

Then he said unto them, Go your way, eat the fat, and drink the sweet, and send portions unto them for whom nothing is prepared: for this day is holy unto our Lord: neither be ye sorry; for the joy of the LORD is your strength. Nehemiah 8:10

The joy of the Lord brings strength and encouragement to those who love and serve Him. No one can take that joy from you when you keep your eyes on Him.

And let us consider one another to provoke unto love and to good works: Hebrews 10:24

Encourage a friend in the Lord. Let's don't be weary in well doing. The Lord is counting on us.

Thou hast proved mine heart; thou hast visited me in the night; thou hast tried me, and shalt find nothing;

I am purposed that my mouth shall not transgress.
Psalm 17:3

Lord, help us all to speak in a way that always brings glory to you and encouragement to others.

The LORD hath done great things for us; whereof we are glad. Psalm 126:3

Don't just think of the difficulties of life. This is a dead-end street. Meditate and be encouraged for what God has done for you. This will make you glad.

There is that speaketh like the piercings of a sword: but the tongue of the wise is health. Proverbs 12:18

What kind of words do we speak? Let's be encouragers.

Thou shalt not raise a false report: put not thine hand with the wicked to be an unrighteous witness.
Exodus 23:1

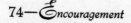

Don't be a slanderer or gossip. Build up and encourage others with your words.

And the LORD visited Sarah as he had said, and the LORD did unto Sarah as he had spoken.
Genesis 21:1

Be encouraged. God always keeps His Word.

Delight thyself also in the LORD; and he shall give thee the desires of thine heart. Psalm 37:4

Get encouragement and joy from your relationship with the Lord. His joy beats anything this world can give.

But Moses' hands were heavy; and they took a stone, and put it under him, and he sat thereon; and Aaron and Hur stayed up his hands, the one on the one side, and the other on the other side; and his hands were steady until the going down of the sun.
Exodus 17:12

Your pastor and other spiritual leaders need your help and encouragement. Be there for them. God will use you.

Now the God of patience and consolation grant you to be likeminded one toward another according to Christ Jesus: That ye may with one mind and one mouth glorify God, even the Father of our Lord Jesus Christ. Wherefore receive ye one another, as Christ also received us to the glory of God.
Romans 15:5-7

May a spirit of unity built upon the Bible arise among God's people today. Let's love and encourage one another.

So they shall make their own tongue to fall upon themselves: all that see them shall flee away.
Psalm 64:8

Gossips will have their pay-day. Be an encourager instead and be a blessing to others and yourself as well.

Faithfulness

But they that wait upon the Lord *shall renew their strength; they shall mount up with wings as eagles; they shall run, and not be weary; and they shall walk, and not faint. Isaiah 40:31*

Live life on the wings of faith in God and watch your life soar to new heights.

Be strong and of a good courage, fear not, nor be afraid of them: for the Lord *thy God, he it is that doth go with thee; he will not fail thee, nor forsake thee. Deuteronomy 31:6*

Faith in God will sustain you through the hard times. Nothing else can compare.

And Jesus called a little child unto him, and set him in the midst of them, And said, Verily I say unto you, Except ye be converted, and become as little children, ye shall not enter into the kingdom of heaven. Matthew 18:2-3

You must have the faith of a child to become a child of God. Have you put your faith in Jesus?

Behold the fowls of the air: for they sow not, neither do they reap, nor gather into barns; yet your heavenly Father feedeth them. Are ye not much better than they? Which of you by taking thought can add one cubit unto his stature? Matthew 6:26-27

Worry is a waste of time and energy. Faith in God is very worthwhile.

I have fought a good fight, I have finished my course, I have kept the faith: 2 Timothy 4:7

Help us, Lord, to be faithful like this. May we never quit. May we be true and faithful until you call us home.

*Yet if any man suffer as a Christian, let him not be
ashamed; but let him glorify God on this behalf.*
1 Peter 4:16

Suffering for the name of Jesus can be a witness and
blessing to others. Stay faithful to the One who gave
His all for you.

*And said unto the woman, Now we believe, not
because of thy saying: for we have heard him
ourselves, and know that this is indeed the Christ,
the Saviour of the world. John 4:42*

Faith in the Lord must be personal. You cannot ride on
the spiritual coattails of someone else. Have you personally put your faith in Jesus?

*In God have I put my trust: I will not be afraid
what man can do unto me. Psalm 56:11*

Faith in God can eliminate the fears we face. Let's put
our total confidence in God.

*That the trial of your faith, being much more
precious than of gold that perisheth, though it be
tried with fire, might be found unto praise and
honour and glory at the appearing of Jesus Christ:
1 Peter 1:7*

A living faith in Jesus is more important than any gold
or silver. Nourish your faith.

*If it be so, our God whom we serve is able to
deliver us from the burning fiery furnace, and he
will deliver us out of thine hand, O king. But if not,
be it known unto thee, O king, that we will not serve
thy gods, nor worship the golden image which thou
hast set up. Daniel 3:17-18*

We need faith like Shadrach, Meshach, and Abednego
today. Let's stand up for the Lord without compromise.

*Commit thy way unto the LORD; trust also in him;
and he shall bring it to pass. Psalm 37:5*

Faith in God is a wise investment. Trust Him to meet
the needs of your life.

They profess that they know God; but in works they deny him, being abominable, and disobedient, and unto every good work reprobate. Titus 1:16

We are saved by faith in Christ. Our faith will produce good works. Do you have real faith in Christ?

Then came the disciples to Jesus apart, and said, Why could not we cast him out? And Jesus said unto them, Because of your unbelief: for verily I say unto you, If ye have faith as a grain of mustard seed, ye shall say unto this mountain, Remove hence to yonder place; and it shall remove; and nothing shall be impossible unto you. Matthew 17:19-20

Faith in Jesus will help you to tackle the impossible too. Have faith in God.

And were continually in the temple, praising and blessing God. Amen. Luke 24:53

People who love Jesus are not looking for excuses not to go to church, but rather they are looking for reasons to go to church. Be faithful in worship.

But Jesus turned him about, and when he saw her, he said, Daughter, be of good comfort; thy faith hath made thee whole. And the woman was made whole from that hour. Matthew 9:22

To experience God's power in our lives we must believe. Put all the faith you've got into the hands of God. You'll be glad you did.

Confidence in an unfaithful man in time of trouble is like a broken tooth, and a foot out of joint. Proverbs 25:19

Can God and others count on you or are you undependable? We need more faithful and dependable people.

If ye be reproached for the name of Christ, happy are ye; for the spirit of glory and of God resteth upon you: on their part he is evil spoken of, but on your part he is glorified. 1 Peter 4:14

If you are being persecuted or ostracized for your commitment to Christ, the joy of the Lord will be your strength. Continue to be faithful to Him.

*And Jesus said unto him, No man, having put his
hand to the plough, and looking back, is fit
for the kingdom of God. Luke 9:62*

Becoming Jesus' disciple requires faithfulness to
Him. Being a Christian is a lifestyle not just something you do.

*And ye shall serve the LORD your God, and he shall
bless thy bread, and thy water; and I will take
sickness away from the midst of thee. Exodus 23:25*

Faithfulness to God has its blessings. Serve the Lord
with gladness and see what He will do in your life.

For we walk by faith, not by sight: 2 Corinthians 5:7

Faith pleases Jesus. Lean on Him. Live by faith.
"Faith is the victory."

*For I know that my redeemer liveth, and that he shall
stand at the latter day upon the earth: And though*

after my skin worms destroy this body, yet in my flesh shall I see God: Job 19:25-26

Real people of God have confidence in the Lord regardless of their circumstances. This is real faith.

Thou shalt make no covenant with them, nor with their gods. Exodus 23:32

No matter how appealing, don't compromise your commitment to the Lord. God will bless your faithfulness to Him.

Because the foolishness of God is wiser than men; and the weakness of God is stronger than men. 1 Corinthians 1:25

Who does this verse make you want to trust? I'm putting my faith in God.

And Jesus answering saith unto them, Have faith in God. Mark 11:22

When all seems lost repeat this verse. God honors faith.

He that loveth father or mother more than me is not worthy of me: and he that loveth son or daughter more than me is not worthy of me. Matthew 10:37

The call to follow Jesus demands faithful commitment. What kind of disciples are we?

And he did not many mighty works there because of their unbelief. Matthew 13:58

Is Jesus being limited in our lives because of our lack of faith in Him? Let's have faith in God.

A righteous man falling down before the wicked is as a troubled fountain, and a corrupt spring. Proverbs 25:26

Don't give up, Christian. Don't give in to compromise. Be strong in the Lord.

But without faith it is impossible to please him: for he that cometh to God must believe that he is, and that he is a rewarder of them that diligently seek him. Hebrews 11:6

Faith in the historical fact that Jesus died on the cross for our sins will bring wonderful salvation. You can't please God without this kind of faith.

And they continued stedfastly in the apostles' doctrine and fellowship, and in breaking of bread, and in prayers. Acts 2:42

There is much to be said for a faithful, consistent walk with God. Be steadfast for the glory of God.

That your faith should not stand in the wisdom of men, but in the power of God. 1 Corinthians 2:5

Real faith is not a matter of just knowing facts but knowing the power of God behind the facts. This faith will see you through the storms of life.

What shall we then say to these things? If God be for us, who can be against us? Romans 8:31

If you are facing tough times because you are faithful to Jesus, remember this verse.

And the things that thou hast heard of me among many witnesses, the same commit thou to faithful men, who shall be able to teach others also. Thou therefore endure hardness, as a good soldier of Jesus Christ. 2 Timothy 2:2-3

Christians are enlisted in God's army. There is a great spiritual battle taking place. Seek to please Jesus.

But I will tarry at Ephesus until Pentecost. For a great door and effectual is opened unto me, and there are many adversaries. 1 Corinthians 16:8-9

When God does a work in your life, you can expect opposition. Don't let the enemy stop you. Have faith in God and keep being faithful.

They shall put you out of the synagogues: yea, the time cometh, that whosoever killeth you will think that he doeth God service. John 16:2

Don't fret if you are persecuted for your faith in Jesus. Jesus said we would face opposition but He also said that He would give us strength to overcome.

Now when Daniel knew that the writing was signed, he went into his house; and his windows being open in his chamber toward Jerusalem, he kneeled upon his knees three times a day, and prayed, and gave thanks before his God, as he did aforetime.
Daniel 6:10

Daniel prayed, knowing that he might face persecution because of his faith. Oh, how we need more men and women with godly convictions. Serve the Lord no matter what the cost.

His lord said unto him, Well done, thou good and faithful servant: thou hast been faithful over a few things, I will make thee ruler over many things: enter thou into the joy of thy lord. Matthew 25:21

It's going to be a wonderful day when we hear the Lord voice His approval about our faithfulness. "Be not weary in well-doing." Keep going for the Lord.

It is better to trust in the LORD than to put confidence in man. It is better to trust in the LORD than to put confidence in princes. Psalm 118:8-9

God is faithful and dependable. Put your trust in Him.

He that is faithful in that which is least is faithful also in much: and he that is unjust in the least is unjust also in much. Luke 16:10

How we handle the details of life also reflects how we will probably handle the larger matters of life. Be faithful to give your best in all that you do.

And he came to the second, and said likewise. And he answered and said, I go, sir: and went not. Matthew 21:30

God is more interested in our actions than our wishful thinking. Be real for God. Follow through in commitments made to Him. Remember, He has been faithful to you.

And immediately the Spirit driveth him into the wilderness. Mark 1:12

Sometimes the Holy Spirit leads us into times of testing to increase our faith. If you're there, hang on to Jesus. He has all the strength you need.

Better is the end of a thing than the beginning thereof: and the patient in spirit is better than the proud in spirit. Ecclesiastes 7:8

Don't quit on God. Finish the race. Complete the course. Remember, the end of the matter is better than the beginning.

And let us not be weary in well doing: for in due season we shall reap, if we faint not. Galatians 6:9

Don't give up. Be faithful to the Lord. You will reap that harvest in time.

But ye, brethren, be not weary in well doing.
2 Thessalonians 3:13

Your work for the Lord is worth it. Keep going. It has eternal significance.

And Peter answered him and said, Lord, if it be thou, bid me come unto thee on the water. And he said, Come. And when Peter was come down out of the ship, he walked on the water, to go to Jesus. But when he saw the wind boisterous, he was afraid; and beginning to sink, he cried, saying, Lord, save me. And immediately Jesus stretched forth his hand, and caught him, and said unto him, O thou of little faith, wherefore didst thou doubt?
Matthew 14:28-31

To obey Jesus we must always keep our eyes of faith upon Jesus.

Be strong and courageous, be not afraid nor dismayed for the king of Assyria, nor for all the multitude that is with him: for there be more with us than with him: With him is an arm of flesh; but with us is the LORD our God to help us, and to fight our battles. And the people rested themselves upon the words of Hezekiah king of Judah.
2 Chronicles 32:7-8

The odds are good for us when we walk with God. Don't be afraid or discouraged by the enemy. Trust in the Lord.

Yea, and all that will live godly in Christ Jesus shall suffer persecution. 2 Timothy 3:12

Devoted Christian, don't be surprised if you suffer persecution for your commitment to Jesus. You're in great company with the men and women of the Bible.

The wicked plotteth against the just, and gnasheth upon him with his teeth. The Lord shall laugh at him: for he seeth that his day is coming.
Psalm 37:12-13

Don't give up, faithful child of God. God will have the last say concerning the righteous and ungodly.

If thou hast run with the footmen, and they have wearied thee, then how canst thou contend with horses? and if in the land of peace, wherein thou trustedst, they wearied thee, then how wilt thou do in the swelling of Jordan? Jeremiah 12:5

If you're commitment level to the Lord is hallow in the good times, how will you be able to stand when times get tough? Strengthen your faith today. "So then faith cometh by hearing, and hearing by the word of God." (Romans 10:17)

Wherefore seeing we also are compassed about with so great a cloud of witnesses, let us lay aside every weight, and the sin which doth so easily beset us, and let us run with patience the race that is set before us, Hebrews 12:1

Christian men have run this race and handed us the baton of faith. Don't drop it. Be faithful.

But ye, brethren, be not weary in well doing.
2 Thessalonians 3:13

Don't quit. Keep going for the Lord. God is depending on you and others need you.

But, beloved, remember ye the words which were
spoken before of the apostles of our Lord Jesus
Christ; How that they told you there should be
mockers in the last time, who should walk after
their own ungodly lusts. Jude 1:17-18

Don't be surprised if you are ridiculed for loving God and His ways. Keep going for Jesus. You will be the winner.

Forgiveness

The heart is deceitful above all things, and
desperately wicked: who can know it?
Jeremiah 17:9

This verse really tells us of our need for the Lord.
Only He can forgive your sins and make you new.

Remember these, O Jacob and Israel; for thou art
my servant: I have formed thee; thou art my servant:
O Israel, thou shalt not be forgotten of me. I have
blotted out, as a thick cloud, thy transgressions, and,
as a cloud, thy sins: return unto me; for I have
redeemed thee. Isaiah 44:21-22

Oh how wonderful it is to know the Lord and His forgiveness. Don't let sin and guilt drag you down. Allow
the Lord to cleanse and forgive you. Do it now!

*For I will be merciful to their unrighteousness, and
their sins and their iniquities will I remember no
more. Hebrews 8:12*

Our great God, the all-knowing One, is willing to forgive and forget. Let go of the past and walk into God's
glorious present and future. He's waiting for you.

*To the Lord our God belong mercies and
forgivenesses, though we have rebelled against him;
Daniel 9:9*

The Lord is more than willing to forgive if we are
ready to repent. The Lord came to save us from our
sin, not in our sin.

*Come now, and let us reason together, saith the
LORD: though your sins be as scarlet, they shall be
as white as snow; though they be red like crimson,
they shall be as wool. Isaiah 1:18*

The Lord will completely wipe our sins away if we let
Him. Have you experienced His forgiveness?

Then came Peter to him, and said, Lord, how oft shall my brother sin against me, and I forgive him? till seven times? Jesus saith unto him, I say not unto thee, Until seven times: but, Until seventy times seven. Matthew 18:21-22

Since the Lord has forgiven us we must be willing to forgive others. This is real Christianity.

Blessed is he whose transgression is forgiven, whose sin is covered. Blessed is the man unto whom the LORD imputeth not iniquity, and in whose spirit there is no guile. Psalm 32:1-2

Thank the Lord for His wonderful forgiveness. You don't have to carry that load of guilt. Confess your sins before the Lord and experience His forgiveness.

*Let all bitterness, and wrath, and anger, and clamour, and evil speaking, be put away from you, with all malice: And be ye kind one to another, tenderhearted, forgiving one another, even as God for Christ's sake hath forgiven you.
Ephesians 4:31-32*

Anger and bitterness stored in your heart will destroy you. Let go of it. Forgive and let the love of the Lord fill your heart.

When Jesus heard it, he saith unto them, They that are whole have no need of the physician, but they that are sick: I came not to call the righteous, but sinners to repentance. Mark 2:17

Jesus loves you. He can and will forgive the sins of the past if you let Him.

For whosoever shall keep the whole law, and yet offend in one point, he is guilty of all. James 2:10

There's no way around it. In God's eyes, at best, we are all sinners. Will you ask Him to forgive you now?

*I, even I, am he that blotteth out thy transgressions for mine own sake, and will not remember thy sins.
Isaiah 43:25*

Only God can forgive sin completely. Have you experienced this? If not, ask the Lord to forgive you. He can make you new.

Be it known unto you therefore, men and brethren, that through this man is preached unto you the forgiveness of sins: Acts 13:38

Forgiveness of sins comes only by trusting Jesus as your Savior. If you're tired of carrying the guilt and burden of your sin, ask Jesus to forgive and cleanse you.

And one cried unto another, and said, Holy, holy, holy, is the LORD of hosts: the whole earth is full of his glory. Isaiah 6:3

God is holy and therefore perfect in all His attributes. There is no way that we will ever spend eternity with Him unless we receive His forgiveness and cleansing of our sins. Have you put your trust in the Lord?

He will turn again, he will have compassion upon us; he will subdue our iniquities; and thou wilt cast all their sins into the depths of the sea. Micah 7:19

The forgiveness of God is totally complete. Ask His forgiveness for your sins and experience a life that is set free from sin's power in your life.

I will therefore that men pray every where, lifting up holy hands, without wrath and doubting.
1 Timothy 2:8

It's difficult to have holy hearts and hands where there is anger and bitterness in our lives. Allow God's love and forgiveness to replace that anger in your life.

But as many as received him, to them gave he power to become the sons of God, even to them that believe on his name: John 1:12

Jesus will forgive you of your sins if you will put your life into His hands. He loves you.

And be ye kind one to another, tenderhearted,
forgiving one another, even as God for Christ's sake
hath forgiven you. Ephesians 4:32

Tenderness and forgiveness are wonderful healers for broken relationships. Remember the love that Jesus has shared with you and share it with another.

Moreover the law entered, that the offence might
abound. But where sin abounded, grace did much
more abound: Romans 5:20

God's grace is greater than any sin you will ever commit. He is able to forgive all sin. Let Him be Lord of your life. Know the joy of total forgiveness.

Be ye angry, and sin not: let not the sun go down
upon your wrath: Ephesians 4:26

Anger that is allowed to build in our lives will not destroy the other person but rather it will destroy us. Ask the Lord to help you to forgive and forget. Resolve your anger before this day is over.

And he said unto her, Thy sins are forgiven.
Luke 7:48

What Jesus said to this woman can be said to you. Repent and let Jesus cleanse and forgive you. Only He can forgive sin.

For the wrath of man worketh not the righteousness of God. James 1:20

An individual filled with anger and bitterness is not much help to the Lord. Ask for God's cleansing and forgiveness and be a real instrument in the hands of God.

But if ye forgive not men their trespasses, neither will your Father forgive your trespasses.
Matthew 6:15

To be forgiven is wonderful; to forgive is just as great. Don't let bitterness and resentment ruin your life. Experience God's forgiveness and forgive others.

As it is written, There is none righteous, no, not one:
Romans 3:10

Every man stands in need of God's forgiveness. No one gets to Heaven on his own merits. Everyone needs the Lord.

As far as the east is from the west, so far hath he removed our transgressions from us. Psalm 103:12

It's great to be forgiven by the Lord. He forgives and removes our sins totally from us. Have you experienced His wonderful forgiveness?

If we confess our sins, he is faithful and just to forgive us our sins, and to cleanse us from all unrighteousness. 1 John 1:9

God is willing and able to forgive if we are willing to confess our sin. Let Him forgive you and cleanse you. He can lift the burden of guilt from your shoulders.

*Saying, Blessed are they whose iniquities are
forgiven, and whose sins are covered. Blessed is the
man to whom the Lord will not impute sin.*
Romans 4:7-8

It's wonderful to be forgiven in the Lord. Confess
your sins to Him and experience His peace.

*If thou, LORD, shouldest mark iniquities, O Lord,
who shall stand? But there is forgiveness with thee,
that thou mayest be feared. Psalm 130:3-4*

Thank the Lord for His wonderful forgiveness.

*And rend your heart, and not your garments, and
turn unto the LORD your God: for he is gracious and
merciful, slow to anger, and of great kindness, and
repenteth him of the evil. Joel 2:13*

The Lord is willing to forgive if you are willing to
repent. He loves you.

Who is a God like unto thee, that pardoneth iniquity,
and passeth by the transgression of the remnant of
his heritage? he retaineth not his anger for ever,
because he delighteth in mercy. Micah 7:18

The Lord longs to pardon and forgive those who come to Him. He loves you.

And, behold, they brought to him a man sick of the
palsy, lying on a bed: and Jesus seeing their faith
said unto the sick of the palsy; Son, be of good
cheer; thy sins be forgiven thee. Matthew 9:2

Only Jesus can forgive our sins. Place your faith in Him. He will cleanse you and make you a new person.

For from within, out of the heart of men, proceed evil
thoughts, adulteries, fornications, murders, thefts,
covetousness, wickedness, deceit, lasciviousness,
an evil eye, blasphemy. Mark 7:21-22

Is it no wonder that we need forgiveness and cleansing for the needy condition of our hearts? Jesus came to set us free.

God's Character

Who is a God like unto thee, that pardoneth iniquity, and passeth by the transgression of the remnant of his heritage? he retaineth not his anger for ever, because he delighteth in mercy. Micah 7:18

Yes, God is holy, but He is also merciful.

Now unto him that is able to do exceeding abundantly above all that we ask or think, according to the power that worketh in us, Unto him be glory in the church by Christ Jesus throughout all ages, world without end. Amen. Ephesians 3:20-21

Our God is great and He is able to do more than we ever dreamed. Have faith in God.

Remember the former things of old: for I am God, and there is none else; I am God, and there is none like me. Isaiah 46:9

There is only one God. His name is the Lord. Put your trust in Him.

But unto them which are called, both Jews and Greeks, Christ the power of God, and the wisdom of God. 1 Corinthians 1:24

Jesus is the power and wisdom of God. He is God. He is the Savior of all who trust Him. Everyone needs Jesus. Do you know Him?

And, behold, this day I am going the way of all the earth: and ye know in all your hearts and in all your souls, that not one thing hath failed of all the good things which the LORD your God spake concerning you; all are come to pass unto you, and not one thing hath failed thereof. Joshua 23:14

God is faithful. He always keeps His promises.

He that is slow to wrath is of great understanding:
but he that is hasty of spirit exalteth folly.
Proverbs 14:29

Patience is a wonderful virtue. Ask the Lord to help you nurture that virtue. Let's don't forget how God has been so patient with us.

God is not a man, that he should lie; neither the son of man, that he should repent: hath he said, and shall he not do it? or hath he spoken, and shall he not make it good? Numbers 23:19

Repeat after me: I can depend on God! He is true to His Word. He can deliver on His promises.

Let them praise the name of the Lord: for he commanded, and they were created.

I thought I would just remind you of the greatness of God. Give Him that burden that you carry. He is able to help you too.

And they remembered that God was their rock, and
the high God their redeemer. Psalm 78:35

Are we ready to remember the Lord? He is our foundation. Without Him there is no hope.

Lord, thou hast been our dwelling place in all
generations. Before the mountains were brought
forth, or ever thou hadst formed the earth and the
world, even from everlasting to everlasting, thou art
God. Psalm 90:1-2

There is only one God. He is the Lord. Place your life in the hands of the great eternal God. He loves you.

Through faith we understand that the worlds were
framed by the word of God, so that things which are
seen were not made of things which do appear.
Hebrews 11:3

Only God could create something out of nothing. We serve a great and all-powerful God.

When my father and my mother forsake me, then the
LORD will take me up. Psalm 27:10

The point is this: God is dependable! Do you feel that
no one cares? He does. Call on Him now to help you.

And God said unto Moses, I AM THAT I AM: and he
said, Thus shalt thou say unto the children of Israel,
I AM hath sent me unto you. Exodus 3:14

God is no "has been." He is just as great and mighty
today as ever. He is the great "I Am." Trust Him with
your life.

For unto us a child is born, unto us a son is given:
and the government shall be upon his shoulder: and
his name shall be called Wonderful, Counsellor, The
mighty God, The everlasting Father, The Prince of
Peace. Isaiah 9:6

Jesus fulfilled this promise. He is still our Wonderful
Counselor, the mighty God, the everlasting Father and
Prince of Peace.

But cursed be the deceiver, which hath in his flock a male, and voweth, and sacrificeth unto the Lord a corrupt thing: for I am a great King, saith the LORD of hosts, and my name is dreadful among the heathen. Malachi 1:14

You can't cheat God and get away with it. The Lord is the Judge of all.

And he saith unto them, Why are ye fearful, O ye of little faith? Then he arose, and rebuked the winds and the sea; and there was a great calm. But the men marvelled, saying, What manner of man is this, that even the winds and the sea obey him! Matthew 8:26-27

Jesus can calm the storms of your life. He's more than a man. He is God the Son.

He saith unto them, But whom say ye that I am? And Simon Peter answered and said, Thou art the Christ, the Son of the living God. Matthew 16:15-16

Jesus was not just a good man, He is the Christ, the Son of the living God. Do you know the Jesus of the Bible?

*Thou art the God that doest wonders: thou hast
declared thy strength among the people.
Psalm 77:14*

We serve a "great, big, wonderful God." He's bigger
than any problem we face.

*Know therefore that the LORD thy God, he is God,
the faithful God, which keepeth covenant and mercy
with them that love him and keep his commandments
to a thousand generations. Deuteronomy 7:9*

You don't have to worry about God keeping His
promise. He is the true and faithful One.

*For, lo, he that formeth the mountains, and createth
the wind, and declareth unto man what is his
thought, that maketh the morning darkness, and
treadeth upon the high places of the earth, The
LORD, The God of hosts, is his name. Amos 4:13*

God is bigger than any problem you have. "With God
nothing is impossible."

Thou shewest lovingkindness unto thousands, and recompensest the iniquity of the fathers into the bosom of their children after them: the Great, the Mighty God, the LORD of hosts, is his name.
Jeremiah 32:18

The Lord loves you! He is so great and yet He is so personal. He cares about you.

Before the mountains were brought forth, or ever thou hadst formed the earth and the world, even from everlasting to everlasting, thou art God.
Psalm 90:2

The Lord is eternal. He does not change. You can depend on Him.

And he saith unto them, But whom say ye that I am? And Peter answereth and saith unto him, Thou art the Christ. Mark 8:29

Jesus is no mere man. He is the Christ, the Son of God. He alone can save man from his sin and its consequences. Have you placed your faith in Him?

*In the beginning God created the heaven
and the earth. Genesis 1:1*

We serve a mighty God. He is bigger than any problem we face. He started this world and He is still on the throne.

*And also the Strength of Israel will not lie nor
repent: for he is not a man, that he should repent.
1 Samuel 15:29*

The Lord is not fickle. He is faithful to do what He says He will do. You can depend on Him.

*I have been young, and now am old; yet have I not
seen the righteous forsaken, nor his seed begging
bread. Psalm 37:25*

God is faithful. "But my God shall supply all your need according to his riches in glory by Christ Jesus." (Philippians 4:19)

He telleth the number of the stars; he calleth them all by their names. Psalm 147:4

We serve a great and mighty God. Remember He is in charge of this world.

As the mountains are round about Jerusalem, so the LORD is round about his people from henceforth even for ever. Psalm 125:2

The Lord is faithful. He will never leave us nor forsake us.

For thy mercy is great above the heavens: and thy truth reacheth unto the clouds. Psalm 108:4

Our Lord is the ultimate in mercy and truth. He's wonderful to know. Praise the Lord.

The LORD also will be a refuge for the oppressed, a refuge in times of trouble. Psalm 9:9

The Lord is that wonderful shelter in the time of the storm. He loves you.

The heavens declare the glory of God; and the firmament sheweth his handywork. Psalm 19:1

Look around you and enjoy God's marvelous creation. We serve a great and mighty God.

But ye shall destroy their altars, break their images, and cut down their groves: For thou shalt worship no other god: for the LORD, whose name is Jealous, is a jealous God: Exodus 34:13-14

The Lord expects and deserves our full worship and obedience. He is worthy to be served.

But he that is greatest among you shall be your servant. And whosoever shall exalt himself shall be abased; and he that shall humble himself shall be exalted. Matthew 23:11-12

Jesus certainly redefines greatness. He lived it too, and so should we.

But God is the judge: he putteth down one, and setteth up another. Psalm 75:7

The Lord is the Judge of all mankind. This is a fact we most certainly need to remember.

They went out from us, but they were not of us; for if they had been of us, they would no doubt have continued with us: but they went out, that they might be made manifest that they were not all of us.
1 John 2:19

Those who really know Jesus stay with Jesus. He's a wonderful Savior.

And they came to him, and awoke him, saying, Master, master, we perish. Then he arose, and rebuked the wind and the raging of the water: and they ceased, and there was a calm. Luke 8:24

Let Jesus calm the storms of your life. Put your circumstances into His capable hands.

Therefore was the wrath of the LORD kindled against his people, insomuch that he abhorred his own inheritance. Psalm 106:40

The anger of God should not be taken lightly. "I tell you, Nay: but, except ye repent, ye shall all likewise perish." (Luke 13:3)

It is better to trust in the LORD than to put confidence in man. Psalm 118:8

You can count on the Lord. He is faithful and dependable.

But the fruit of the Spirit is love, joy, peace, longsuffering, gentleness, goodness, faith, Meekness, temperance: against such there is no law.
Galatians 5:22-23

This is what people who know Jesus should be like.

Jesus Christ the same yesterday, and to day, and for ever. Hebrews 13:8

Jesus is totally reliable. He never changes. Put your life in His hands.

For thy mercy is great above the heavens: and thy truth reacheth unto the clouds. Psalm 108:4

God is great. God is love. God is faithful. You can depend on Him.

God's Goodness

According to their pasture, so were they filled; they were filled, and their heart was exalted; therefore have they forgotten me. Hosea 13:6

Have we taken God and His goodness for granted? If we have, we are the losers. Let's give God the glory for the way He has provided for us.

Only take heed to thyself, and keep thy soul diligently, lest thou forget the things which thine eyes have seen, and lest they depart from thy heart all the days of thy life: but teach them thy sons, and thy sons' sons. Deuteronomy 4:9

Time spent daily in the Bible will help us remember the goodness of the Lord. Be diligent. Don't forget the Lord and His will for your life.

Cease from anger, and forsake wrath: fret not thyself in any wise to do evil. Psalm 37:8

This verse will save you a lot of heartache. Don't waste your energy on anger and worry. Fill your heart with the goodness of the Lord.

Or despisest thou the riches of his goodness and forbearance and longsuffering; not knowing that the goodness of God leadeth thee to repentance? Romans 2:4

Think on the ways God has blessed you. Is there something you want to tell Him? Shouldn't His goodness lead us to honor Him with our lives?

I have been young, and now am old; yet have I not seen the righteous forsaken, nor his seed begging bread. Psalm 37:25

The Lord takes care of His people now and for eternity. Thank you, Lord, for being so good to us.

*They forgat God their saviour, which had done great
things in Egypt. Psalm 106:21*

Don't forget the goodness of God. Those who do rob
themselves of a blessing and peace of mind.

*What shall I render unto the LORD for all his benefits
toward me? Psalm 116:12*

Express your gratitude to the Lord. He is so good!
Now think what you can do to bless Him.

*I remember the days of old; I meditate on all thy
works; I muse on the work of thy hands.
Psalm 143:5*

The forgetting of God's works robs us of many blessings. Take time right now to reflect on the goodness of
God.

*The LORD will give strength unto his people; the
LORD will bless his people with peace. Psalm 29:11*

Strength and peace belong to the people of God. What more could a person want? God is so good.

Every good gift and every perfect gift is from above, and cometh down from the Father of lights, with whom is no variableness, neither shadow of turning.
James 1:17

All good comes from God. Be sure to thank Him for His goodness to you.

Bless the LORD, O my soul, and forget not all his benefits: Who forgiveth all thine iniquities; who healeth all thy diseases; Psalm 103:2-3

God is so good. He has done wonderful works in your life.

And we know that all things work together for good to them that love God, to them who are the called according to his purpose. Romans 8:28

The Lord is always up to good in the lives of those who love him. That sure makes it easy to love our wonderful Lord.

I will remember the works of the LORD: surely I will remember thy wonders of old. I will meditate also of all thy work, and talk of thy doings.
Psalm 77:11-12

Take time to meditate on the Lord and His goodness. This will bless your life. Have a good day.

This is the day which the LORD hath made; we will rejoice and be glad in it. Psalm 118:24

Every day is a gift from God. Make the most of it with God's help.

Bless the LORD, O my soul: and all that is within me, bless his holy name. Bless the LORD, O my soul, and forget not all his benefits: Psalm 103:1-2

Praise the Lord! God is so good to us. Count your blessings.

Whoso rewardeth evil for good, evil shall not depart from his house. Proverbs 17:13

Think twice before you reject the goodness of God. It has its consequences.

The LORD is good, a strong hold in the day of trouble; and he knoweth them that trust in him. Nahum 1:7

Has life beat you down? Go to the Lord. He will comfort and strengthen you.

When thou hast eaten and art full, then thou shalt bless the LORD thy God for the good land which he hath given thee. Deuteronomy 8:10

Have you taken time to thank God for His goodness?

*And we know that all things work together for good
to them that love God, to them who are the called
according to his purpose. Romans 8:28*

God is up to good in the lives of His people. Even the
tough times can be a blessing when we walk with
God.

*Be not overcome of evil, but overcome evil with
good. Romans 12:21*

This is the way Christians are to live. Let's allow
God's goodness to overflow in our lives.

*I love the LORD, because he hath heard my voice and
my supplications. Because he hath inclined his ear
unto me, therefore will I call upon him as long as I
live. Psalm 116:1-2*

Do you love the Lord? We all should. He's been so
good to us.

For the LORD God is a sun and shield: the LORD will give grace and glory: no good thing will he withhold from them that walk uprightly. Psalm 84:11

What a promise. Walk with God and watch His goodness surround your life.

According to their pasture, so were they filled; they were filled, and their heart was exalted; therefore have they forgotten me. Hosea 13:6

Have we taken God and His goodness for granted? If we have, we are the losers. Let's give God the glory for the way He has provided for us.

Every good gift and every perfect gift is from above, and cometh down from the Father of lights, with whom is no variableness, neither shadow of turning. James 1:17

All goodness comes from God. Without Him there would be nothing but bad and evil. We all need the Lord.

*I love the LORD, because he hath heard my voice and
my supplications. Psalm 116:1*

We too should love the Lord because of His goodness
and mercy toward us. Let's live lives that are pleasing
to Him.

Growing in
God's Word

And Jesus answered and said unto them, Take heed that no man deceive you. Matthew 24:4

Compare all that you hear to the Bible. If it doesn't ring true with God's Word, beware.

God is not a man, that he should lie; neither the son of man, that he should repent: hath he said, and shall he not do it? or hath he spoken, and shall he not make it good? Numbers 23:19

God said it and that settles it whether we believe it or not. God can't lie. You can depend on Him and on His Word the Bible.

Search the scriptures; for in them ye think ye have eternal life: and they are they which testify of me.
John 5:39

Are you looking for answers to life and life eternal? Read the Bible. Then you will clearly see that Jesus has the answers to these questions. Put your life into His hands.

And Jesus increased in wisdom and stature, and in favour with God and man. Luke 2:52

Are you growing in the Lord? Take time to pray and read the Bible. Be faithful to worship the Lord in church and wherever you go.

And when these things begin to come to pass, then look up, and lift up your heads; for your redemption draweth nigh. Luke 21:28

Are the rapid changes of this world pointing to something? I think so. Read the Bible and you will begin to understand Jesus' second coming is closer everyday.

He sent his word, and healed them, and delivered
them from their destructions. Psalm 107:20

The Word of God can bring healing to the heart, mind
and body. Read it and believe it.

So Jotham became mighty, because he prepared his
ways before the LORD his God. 2 Chronicles 27:6

Preparation is a key to Godly living. Prepare your
ways before the Lord. Spend time with Him and seek
His wisdom.

Therefore turn thou to thy God: keep mercy and
judgment, and wait on thy God continually.
Hosea 12:6

"Return to the Lord." This is a message much needed
today. Let's heed and obey God's Word.

Sanctify them through thy truth: thy word is truth.
John 17:17

Where can a person find the truth? It's in the Bible. "Thy Word is truth."

Heaven and earth shall pass away: but my words shall not pass away. Luke 21:33

The Word of the Lord is totally reliable. It is timeless. Place your faith in Jesus.

So then faith cometh by hearing, and hearing by the word of God. Romans 10:17

Do you need more faith in God? Read the Bible.

Thy word have I hid in mine heart, that I might not sin against thee. Psalm 119:11

Placing God's Word in our hearts is one of the keys to having victory over temptation. Take time to read the Bible.

Thy word is a lamp unto my feet, and a light unto my path. Psalm 119:105

Are you in the dark about certain decisions? God's Word will light your way.

All scripture is given by inspiration of God, and is profitable for doctrine, for reproof, for correction, for instruction in righteousness: 2 Timothy 3:16

The Bible is not just any book. It is the inspired Word of God. Read it and believe it. It can change your life.

The law of the LORD is perfect, converting the soul: the testimony of the LORD is sure, making wise the simple. Psalm 19:7

The benefits of keeping God's Word are tremendous. Take time to "cash in" on them today.

Heaven and earth shall pass away: but my words shall not pass away. Mark 13:31

You can depend on the Word of the Lord. His Word is eternal.

And he said unto them, Set your hearts unto all the words which I testify among you this day, which ye shall command your children to observe to do, all the words of this law. For it is not a vain thing for you; because it is your life: and through this thing ye shall prolong your days in the land, whither ye go over Jordan to possess it. Deuteronomy 32:46-47

The Word of God is not just a collection of sayings. It is life itself. Happiness comes when we believe it and obey it. Take time to read the Word today.

For when for the time ye ought to be teachers, ye have need that one teach you again which be the first principles of the oracles of God; and are become such as have need of milk, and not of strong meat. Hebrews 5:12

Are you growing in the grace and knowledge of the Lord Jesus? Read God's Word and let Him give you strength and wisdom for each day.

So shall my word be that goeth forth out of my mouth: it shall not return unto me void, but it shall accomplish that which I please, and it shall prosper in the thing whereto I sent it. Isaiah 55:11

There is power in the Word of God. We don't have to defend it. We just need to declare it. God will take care of the rest.

But the word of God grew and multiplied.
Acts 12:24

You can't hold back the powerful impact of the Bible. It is still pointing people to our wonderful Lord.

For the time will come when they will not endure sound doctrine; but after their own lusts shall they heap to themselves teachers, having itching ears; And they shall turn away their ears from the truth, and shall be turned unto fables. 2 Timothy 4:3-4

We must never be guilty of picking and choosing just what we like in God's Word. We must seek to obey the Lord in all our ways.

The grass withereth, the flower fadeth: but the word of our God shall stand for ever. Isaiah 40:8

The Word of God stands forever. You can trust God to keep His Word.

And ye shall seek me, and find me, when ye shall search for me with all your heart. Jeremiah 29:13

Sincerely seek the Lord and you will find Him. Read the Bible daily and learn more about Him.

Behold, ye trust in lying words, that cannot profit. Jeremiah 7:8

The words that really profit mankind are the words of God. Read the Bible. Believe it. You can depend on God to keep His Word.

In hope of eternal life, which God, that cannot lie, promised before the world began; Titus 1:2

God cannot lie. You can depend on Him to keep His Word.

Beware lest any man spoil you through philosophy and vain deceit, after the tradition of men, after the rudiments of the world, and not after Christ.
Colossians 2:8

Keep your eyes on Jesus and His Word. That will protect you from getting side-tracked.

For ever, O LORD, thy word is settled in heaven.
Psalm 119:89

We need not defend the Word of God. We just need to proclaim it and watch God do His mighty and eternal work.

Therefore whosoever heareth these sayings of mine, and doeth them, I will liken him unto a wise man, which built his house upon a rock: Matthew 7:24

Build your life upon the solid rock. Build your life on Jesus and His Word.

But be ye doers of the word, and not hearers only, deceiving your own selves. James 1:22

Real Christians not only know the Word of God but also do the Word of God. Are you for real?

For the prophecy came not in old time by the will of man: but holy men of God spake as they were moved by the Holy Ghost. 2 Peter 1:21

The Bible is the inspired Word of God. You can always depend on His Word.

The Lord gave the word: great was the company of those that published it. Psalm 68:11

The Lord will always have His company to proclaim His Word. God's Word is eternal.

He also that received seed among the thorns is he that heareth the word; and the care of this world, and the deceitfulness of riches, choke the word, and he becometh unfruitful. Matthew 13:22

The cares of this world can rob us of God's blessings. Concentrate on God and His Word. He is the One that makes life worth living.

Heaven and earth shall pass away, but my words shall not pass away. Matthew 24:35

The Word of God is totally reliable. You can depend on Him.

But he that heareth, and doeth not, is like a man that without a foundation built an house upon the earth; against which the stream did beat vehemently, and immediately it fell; and the ruin of that house was great. Luke 6:49

It's not the hearing of God's Word that makes the difference, it's the doing of God's Word that makes faith come alive.

These were more noble than those in Thessalonica, in that they received the word with all readiness of mind, and searched the scriptures daily, whether those things were so. Acts 17:11

Let's be a people of the Bible. Take time to read it.

Behold, the days come, saith the Lord GOD, that I will send a famine in the land, not a famine of bread, nor a thirst for water, but of hearing the words of the LORD. Amos 8:11

Don't take the Word of God for granted. Read it. Heed it. Obey it. Love it.

These things have I written unto you that believe on the name of the Son of God; that ye may know that ye have eternal life, and that ye may believe on the name of the Son of God. 1 John 5:13

God's Word is written down for us so that we can know assuredly that we are secure in Him. You can know you have eternal life because you know Jesus personally.

Be still, and know that I am God: I will be exalted among the heathen, I will be exalted in the earth.
Psalm 46:10

Stop! Get alone with God in the study of the Bible and prayer. It will pay great dividends.

For my thoughts are not your thoughts, neither are your ways my ways, saith the LORD. For as the heavens are higher than the earth, so are my ways higher than your ways, and my thoughts than your thoughts. Isaiah 55:8-9

This is why we must spend time in the Bible and on our knees. We must learn God's ways.

Blessed is he that readeth, and they that hear the words of this prophecy, and keep those things which are written therein: for the time is at hand.
Revelation 1:3

There is a blessing awaiting those who read and heed God's Word. Take time to be blessed today.

O earth, earth, earth, hear the word of the LORD.
Jeremiah 22:29

There can be no more compelling cry than the one above. Take time to seek the Lord.

This book of the law shall not depart out of thy mouth; but thou shalt meditate therein day and night, that thou mayest observe to do according to all that is written therein: for then thou shalt make thy way prosperous, and then thou shalt have good success. Joshua 1:8

Meditate on God's Word and obey God's Word. This is real success.

Then the twelve called the multitude of the disciples unto them, and said, It is not reason that we should leave the word of God, and serve tables. Wherefore, brethren, look ye out among you seven men of honest report, full of the Holy Ghost and wisdom, whom we may appoint over this business. But we will give ourselves continually to prayer, and to the ministry of the word. Acts 6:2-4

It's important that spiritual leaders take time to study the Bible and pray. God's people are depending on these shepherds.

Finally, my brethren, be strong in the Lord, and in the power of his might. Put on the whole armour of God, that ye may be able to stand against the wiles of the devil. Ephesians 6:10-11

There is a spiritual war taking place in our land. God's people must clothe themselves in His armor. Christian, read the Bible and pray and you will be ready.

Now I beseech you, brethren, mark them which cause divisions and offenses contrary to the doctrine which ye have learned; and avoid them. For they that are such serve not our Lord Jesus Christ, but their own belly; and by good words and fair speeches deceive the hearts of the simple. Romans 16:17-18

Make sure that your faith is built upon the Bible and not upon the opinion of others.

And be renewed in the spirit of your mind; And that ye put on the new man, which after God is created in righteousness and true holiness. Ephesians 4:23-24

Christian, are you taking time to be renewed? Read the Bible and pray every day.

Thus saith the LORD, thy Redeemer, the Holy One of Israel; I am the LORD thy God which teacheth thee to profit, which leadeth thee by the way that thou shouldest go. O that thou hadst hearkened to my commandments! then had thy peace been as a river, and thy righteousness as the waves of the sea: Isaiah 48:17-18

The reason we lack the peace of God is because we fail to listen to Him. Take time to let God speak to you through the Bible.

For the word of God is quick, and powerful, and sharper than any twoedged sword, piercing even to the dividing asunder of soul and spirit, and of the joints and marrow, and is a discerner of the thoughts and intents of the heart. Hebrews 4:12

The Bible is the Word of God. Man needs it. The Bible both convicts and comforts. Take time to read it.

For your obedience is come abroad unto all men. I am glad therefore on your behalf: but yet I would have you wise unto that which is good, and simple concerning evil. Romans 16:19

The only way to be wise about good and innocent about evil is to walk with Jesus and follow His ways.

Yet he sent prophets to them, to bring them again unto the LORD; and they testified against them: but they would not give ear. 2 Chronicles 24:19

The people in this scripture would not listen to God's message. How about you? Is your heart open to hear God's Word?

For all flesh is as grass, and all the glory of man as the flower of grass. The grass withereth, and the flower thereof falleth away: But the word of the Lord

endureth for ever. And this is the word which by the
gospel is preached unto you. 1 Peter 1:24-25

You and I will come and go but the Word of God stands forever. You can depend on God's Word.

For thus saith the LORD unto the house of Israel,
Seek ye me, and ye shall live. Amos 5:4

Real life comes to us when we seek the Lord. Get on your knees and open your Bible and seek the Lord now.

Wherewithal shall a young man cleanse his way? by
taking heed thereto according to thy word.
Psalm 119:9

Purity is a virtue that desperately needs to be restored in our world. The way to purity is to follow God's Word.

And I, brethren, could not speak unto you as unto
spiritual, but as unto carnal, even as unto babes in

Christ. I have fed you with milk, and not with meat:
for hitherto ye were not able to bear it, neither yet
now are ye able. 1 Corinthians 3:1-2

Christian, are you growing in Jesus? Take time to read
your Bible and pray. Move forward in your Christian
life.

Now when they saw the boldness of Peter and John,
and perceived that they were unlearned and ignorant
men, they marvelled; and they took knowledge of
them, that they had been with Jesus. Acts 4:13

Christian, can people tell that we have been with
Jesus? Take time to read God's Word and pray every
day.

For laying aside the commandment of God, ye hold
the tradition of men, as the washing of pots and
cups: and many other such like things ye do.
Mark 7:8

Don't let tradition take the place of God's Word in
your life. Stick with the Bible.

And Samuel grew, and the LORD was with him, and did let none of his words fall to the ground.
1 Samuel 3:19

We, too, need to cling to God's Word. It will give us real meaning and wisdom.

This book of the law shall not depart out of thy mouth; but thou shalt meditate therein day and night, that thou mayest observe to do according to all that is written therein: for then thou shalt make thy way prosperous, and then thou shalt have good success. Joshua 1:8

Here's the key to real peace and success. Meditate on God's Word and then obey it.

His Love,
Our Love

And he went a little further, and fell on his face, and prayed, saying, O my Father, if it be possible, let this cup pass from me: nevertheless not as I will, but as thou wilt. Matthew 26:39

Don't forget this. Jesus loved you so much that He voluntarily gave His life for you on the cross.

For though I be free from all men, yet have I made myself servant unto all, that I might gain the more. 1 Corinthians 9:19

Jesus delivers us from the bondage of sin so that we can be free to love ourselves, others, and Him. It's great to be free from sin and selfishness.

I am the good shepherd: the good shepherd giveth his life for the sheep. John 10:11

Don't ever doubt that God loves you. He gave His life for you on Calvary. He gave His life. What more could He give?

But God, who is rich in mercy, for his great love wherewith he loved us, Even when we were dead in sins, hath quickened us together with Christ, (by grace ye are saved;) And hath raised us up together, and made us sit together in heavenly places in Christ Jesus. Ephesians 2:4-6

Why did God send His precious Son to die for us on the cross? He did it because He loves us. Dwell on that thought today. God loves you!

Let nothing be done through strife or vainglory; but in lowliness of mind let each esteem other better than themselves. Philippians 2:3

What are our motives for doing what we do? Let's put aside selfishness ambition and serve one another in real love and humility.

And thou shalt love the Lord thy God with all thy heart, and with all thy soul, and with all thy mind, and with all thy strength: this is the first commandment. Mark 12:30

We are not to love the Lord with a casual commitment. He wants our all. Let's don't forget, He gave His all for us.

I will sing of the mercies of the LORD for ever: with my mouth will I make known thy faithfulness to all generations. Psalm 89:1

God's love and faithfulness are great words for any conversation and any song. "Let the redeemed of the Lord say so."

*But as it is written, Eye hath not seen, nor ear heard, neither have entered into the heart of man, the things which God hath prepared for them that love him.
1 Corinthians 2:9*

God's love for you and me is beyond human understanding and description. He loves us very much.

But speaking the truth in love, may grow up into him
in all things, which is the head, even Christ.
Ephesians 4:15

Yes, speak the truth but speak it always in a spirit of love. You may have a more receptive audience then.

And I will delight myself in thy commandments,
which I have loved. Psalm 119:47

What an attitude! Obey the Lord because you love Him and His commandments. He has your best interest in mind.

He saith to him again the second time, Simon, son of
Jonas, lovest thou me? He saith unto him, Yea, Lord;
thou knowest that I love thee. He saith unto him,
Feed my sheep. John 21:16

Jesus wants to know the extent of our love for Him. He said, "If you love me keep my commandments." How much do you love Him?

*But he was wounded for our transgressions, he was
bruised for our iniquities: the chastisement of our
peace was upon him; and with his stripes we are
healed. All we like sheep have gone astray; we have
turned every one to his own way; and the LORD hath
laid on him the iniquity of us all. Isaiah 53:5-6*

Thank you, Jesus, for what you did for us on the cross.
We will never forget your great love for us.

*And the Word was made flesh, and dwelt among us,
(and we beheld his glory, the glory as of the only
begotten of the Father,) full of grace and truth.
John 1:14*

The greatest miracle recorded in history was when
God became man to become the Savior of the world.
Thank you, Jesus, for your love for us.

*As many as I love, I rebuke and chasten: be zealous
therefore, and repent. Revelation 3:19*

One sign of God's love is His discipline. Realize that
His discipline is for your benefit. He does it because
He loves you.

His Love, Our Love—155

Herein is love, not that we loved God, but that he loved us, and sent his Son to be the propitiation for our sins. 1 John 4:10

God loved us long before we ever thought of loving Him. Remember, Jesus loves you.

All that the Father giveth me shall come to me; and him that cometh to me I will in no wise cast out. John 6:37

Jesus loves you! Have you experienced His love? Come to Him. He will change your life for the better. Love Him and obey Him. You'll be glad you did.

He that saith he is in the light, and hateth his brother, is in darkness even until now. He that loveth his brother abideth in the light, and there is none occasion of stumbling in him. 1 John 2:9-10

Real Christians love one another. Allow the love of Jesus to flow through you.

But as touching brotherly love ye need not that I write unto you: for ye yourselves are taught of God to love one another. 1 Thessalonians 4:9

Even people who don't profess Christ know that Christians are to love one another. Love for others is a powerful testimony of the grace of God.

And above all things have fervent charity among yourselves: for charity shall cover the multitude of sins. 1 Peter 4:8

God's love set loose in our hearts can do mighty miracles. Allow God's love to permeate your life.

Come unto me, all ye that labour and are heavy laden, and I will give you rest. Take my yoke upon you, and learn of me; for I am meek and lowly in heart: and ye shall find rest unto your souls. For my yoke is easy, and my burden is light.
Matthew 11:28-30

Jesus loves you. Unload your burdens on Him. He will give you the rest and strength you need.

Though I speak with the tongues of men and of angels, and have not charity, I am become as sounding brass, or a tinkling cymbal.
1 Corinthians 13:1

Love must be the motivating force for life. Anything else is less than our best.

And thou shalt love the LORD thy God with all thine heart, and with all thy soul, and with all thy might.
Deuteronomy 6:5

The Lord deserves and demands more than a half-hearted devotion. We should love and serve Him with all that we are.

But cleave unto the LORD your God, as ye have done unto this day. Take good heed therefore unto yourselves, that ye love the LORD your God.
Joshua 23:8,11

Love for the Lord and faithfulness to the Lord are key ingredients to effective discipleship. Do you have these key ingredients?

But I say unto you which hear, Love your enemies,
do good to them which hate you. Luke 6:27

Jesus can give us the strength to do these things. Let love flow.

But God commendeth his love toward us, in that,
while we were yet sinners, Christ died for us.
Romans 5:8

Jesus loves you. Say that to yourself. It's the greatest news this world has ever heard.

LORD, thou hast heard the desire of the humble: thou
wilt prepare their heart, thou wilt cause thine ear to
hear. Psalm 10:17

The Lord loves His people. Tell Him the needs of your life.

Hatred stirreth up strifes: but love covereth all sins.
Proverbs 10:12

Hatred destroys. Love heals. Be a healer.

*For the love of Christ constraineth us; because we
thus judge, that if one died for all, then were all
dead. 2 Corinthians 5:14*

Service for the Lord should not be out of guilt, but
rather out of love for Jesus and others.

*This is my commandment, That ye love one another,
as I have loved you. John 15:12*

Loving each other as Christians is not an option, it's a
command. Because Jesus loves us we can love each
other.

*For the LORD taketh pleasure in his people: he will
beautify the meek with salvation. Psalm 149:4*

The Lord loves His people. His salvation is a by-prod-
uct of His love. Have you committed your life to the
Lord?

And now abideth faith, hope, charity, these three;
but the greatest of these is charity.
1 Corinathians 13:13

The love of God is the greatest power in all the world.
Let His love overflow your heart.

For, brethren, ye have been called unto liberty; only
use not liberty for an occasion to the flesh, but by
love serve one another. Galatians 5:13

Jesus has set us free so that we can serve Him and others. Love Him and others and experience real life.

I love the LORD, because he hath heard my voice and
my supplications. Because he hath inclined his ear
unto me, therefore will I call upon him as long as I
live. Psalm 116:1-2

Loving the Lord is the proper response to who He is
and what He has done for us. Live a life that pleases
Him.

Jesus Christ the same yesterday, and to day, and for ever. Hebrews 13:8

Jesus never changes. He never stops loving His children. You can depend on Him.

O give thanks unto the LORD; for he is good: for his mercy endureth for ever. O give thanks unto the God of gods: for his mercy endureth for ever. Psalm 136:1-2

God's love has no end. He loves His people with an everlasting love.

Master, which is the great commandment in the law? Jesus said unto him, Thou shalt love the Lord thy God with all thy heart, and with all thy soul, and with all thy mind. This is the first and great commandment. And the second is like unto it, Thou shalt love thy neighbour as thyself. Matthew 22:36-39

This is real Christianity. Let's allow Jesus' love to flow through us. Everyone needs to be loved.

For I desired mercy, and not sacrifice; and the knowledge of God more than burnt offerings.
Hosea 6:6

The Lord is more interested in our sincerity of love for Him than our rituals. Have a genuine love for God.

If ye love me, keep my commandments. John 14:15

If we truly love Jesus, we will want to obey Him. Can others tell we love Jesus?

The LORD is my light and my salvation; whom shall I fear? the LORD is the strength of my life; of whom shall I be afraid? Psalm 27:1

God's presence and love will drive fear out of your life. Place your life in God's hands.

For they verily for a few days chastened us after their own pleasure; but he for our profit, that we might be partakers of his holiness. Hebrews 12:10

God disciplines us because He loves us. If He didn't, we wouldn't be His.

Be merciful unto me, O God, be merciful unto me: for my soul trusteth in thee: yea, in the shadow of thy wings will I make my refuge, until these calamities be overpast. Psalm 57:1

You too can take refuge under God's care. He loves you.

Come now, and let us reason together, saith the LORD: though your sins be as scarlet, they shall be as white as snow; though they be red like crimson, they shall be as wool. Isaiah 1:18

The Lord can remove the sin and guilt of your life. He loves you.

For ye know the grace of our Lord Jesus Christ, that, though he was rich, yet for your sakes he became poor, that ye through his poverty might be rich.
2 Corinthians 8:9

How much does Jesus love you? He loves you enough to leave the splendor of Heaven to die on a cross for you. That's real love.

If a man say, I love God, and hateth his brother, he is a liar: for he that loveth not his brother whom he hath seen, how can he love God whom he hath not seen? 1 John 4:20

Christian love is real. Since Jesus loves us, we can love each other.

Ye that love the LORD, hate evil: he preserveth the souls of his saints; he delivereth them out of the hand of the wicked. Psalm 97:10

When we really love the Lord we will hate evil. Love the Lord with all your heart. He will guard your life.

My little children, let us not love in word, neither in tongue; but in deed and in truth. 1 John 3:18

Love is more than words. It's action. Show the Lord and someone else today that you love them.

Ye that love the LORD, hate evil: he preserveth the souls of his saints; he delivereth them out of the hand of the wicked. Psalm 97:10

God loves you. He gave His Son, Jesus, for you. Give your life to the One who loves you. Give your life to the Lord.

In my distress I cried unto the LORD, and he heard me. Psalm 120:1

Call on the Lord. He loves you and can help you. Submit your life to Him.

Now before the feast of the passover, when Jesus knew that his hour was come that he should depart out of this world unto the Father, having loved his own which were in the world, he loved them unto the end. John 13:1

Don't ever doubt Jesus' love for you. His love sent Him to the cross for you.

Nevertheless I have somewhat against thee, because thou hast left thy first love. Revelation 2:4

Oh Christian, do you love Jesus? Here's how to know you do. "If ye love me, keep my commandments." (John 14:15)

Humility

He hath shewed thee, O man, what is good; and
what doth the LORD require of thee, but to do justly,
and to love mercy, and to walk humbly with thy
God? Micah 6:8

Justice, mercy, and humility are still characteristics of the people of the Lord. Are people seeing the Lord in us?

He hath shewed thee, O man, what is good; and
what doth the LORD require of thee, but to do
justly, and to love mercy, and to walk
humbly with thy God? Micah 6:8

How are you doing in the requirements of the Lord? Justice, humility, and mercy should be the trademark of people who know the Lord.

Restore unto me the joy of thy salvation; and uphold me with thy free spirit. Psalm 51:12

God will restore His joy if we will just humble ourselves before Him.

*But when he was strong, his heart was lifted up to his destruction: for he transgressed against the LORD his God, and went into the temple of the LORD to burn incense upon the altar of incense.
2 Chronicles 26:16*

Pride will bring you down, not up.

Because thine heart was tender, and thou didst humble thyself before God, when thou heardest his words against this place, and against the inhabitants thereof, and humbledst thyself before me, and didst rend thy clothes, and weep before me; I have even heard thee also, saith the LORD. 2 Chronicles 34:27

Is your heart humbled before God? God can work in the hearts of those who weep over things that make God weep.

Pride goeth before destruction, and an haughty spirit before a fall. Proverbs 16:18

Pride is a great deceiver. Put your trust and confidence in the Lord and not in yourself or things.

Though the LORD be high, yet hath he respect unto the lowly: but the proud he knoweth afar off. Psalm 138:6

True humility finds favor with God. Pride is a barrier to our walk with God. Which controls your life, pride or humility?

And men were scorched with great heat, and blasphemed the name of God, which hath power over these plagues: and they repented not to give him glory. Revelation 16:9

In the last days men will know that God is judging them and yet they will refuse to repent. The longer you wait to surrender to God the bigger your pride becomes.

But when he was strong, his heart was lifted up to his destruction: for he transgressed against the LORD his God, and went into the temple of the LORD to burn incense upon the altar of incense.
2 Chronicles 26:16

Don't let strength and pride be your downfall. Walk humbly before the Lord.

Your glorying is not good. Know ye not that a little leaven leaveneth the whole lump? 1 Corinthians 5:6

Pride can be a terrible master. It's foolish for a man to think he can face this life and the life to come without the Lord.

For I say, through the grace given unto me, to every man that is among you, not to think of himself more highly than he ought to think; but to think soberly, according as God hath dealt to every man the measure of faith. Romans 12:3

The world does not revolve around you and me. It's a humbling thought but a good one to help us keep all things in perspective.

For whosoever exalteth himself shall be abased; and
he that humbleth himself shall be exalted.
Luke 14:11

This is just the opposite from the teaching of this world. Don't forget, however, that God always has the last word. Humble yourself before God and others and He will exalt you.

Behold, this was the iniquity of thy sister Sodom,
pride, fulness of bread, and abundance of idleness
was in her and in her daughters, neither did she
strengthen the hand of the poor and needy.
Ezekiel 16:49

We are prime candidates for selfishness when we have it all. If God has blessed you, realize that it all comes from Him.

But he giveth more grace. Wherefore he saith, God
resisteth the proud, but giveth grace unto the
humble. James 4:6

When pride fills your life you will be fighting an uphill battle against the Lord. Humble yourself before

God and let Him shower you with His grace and blessings.

Then saith Pilate unto him, Speakest thou not unto me? knowest thou not that I have power to crucify thee, and have power to release thee? Jesus answered, Thou couldest have no power at all against me, except it were given thee from above: John 19:10-11

We are not as high and mighty as we may think. Don't forget that God has the last word. Don't be His enemy. Be His servant.

And the loftiness of man shall be bowed down, and the haughtiness of men shall be made low: and the LORD alone shall be exalted in that day. Isaiah 2:17

Human pride is no match for the glory of God. Don't put your trust in self. Put your trust in the Lord. When it's all said and done, "the Lord alone shall be exalted."

But Peter said unto him, Thy money perish with thee, because thou hast thought that the gift of God may be purchased with money. Acts 8:20

Money cannot buy favor from God. He's looking for people with humble hearts that will simply obey Him.

The pride of thine heart hath deceived thee, thou that dwellest in the clefts of the rock, whose habitation is high; that saith in his heart, Who shall bring me down to the ground? Obadiah 1:3

How many times have we deceived ourselves by putting our trust in our own foolish pride?

For thus saith the high and lofty One that inhabiteth eternity, whose name is Holy; I dwell in the high and holy place, with him also that is of a contrite and humble spirit, to revive the spirit of the humble, and to revive the heart of the contrite ones. Isaiah 57:15

Humility is a necessary ingredient in walking with the Lord. Don't let pride keep you from Him.

*And Gideon said unto them, I will not rule over you,
neither shall my son rule over you: the LORD shall
rule over you. Judges 8:23*

Godly leadership is marked by humility and loving
service.

*Ye blind guides, which strain at a gnat, and swallow
a camel. Matthew 23:24*

While we are so busy straining out the insignificant in
our lives we are being eaten alive by godlessness and
immorality. Let's get priorities straight. Let's humble
ourselves and seek the will of God.

*And when he was in affliction, he besought the LORD
his God, and humbled himself greatly before the God
of his fathers, And prayed unto him: and he was
intreated of him, and heard his supplication, and
brought him again to Jerusalem into his kingdom.
Then Manasseh knew that the LORD he was God.
2 Chronicles 33:12-13*

God will never do a great work in our lives until we
humble ourselves before Him.

Yea, truth faileth; and he that departeth from evil
maketh himself a prey: and the LORD saw it, and it
displeased him that there was no judgment.
Isaiah 59:15

I imagine that the Lord is as displeased with our world
today as He was back then. Where is justice? Where
is truth? We will never recapture these values until we
humble ourselves before the Lord.

Forasmuch as ye know that ye were not redeemed
with corruptible things, as silver and gold, from your
vain conversation received by tradition from your
fathers; But with the precious blood of Christ, as of
a lamb without blemish and without spot:
1 Peter 1:18-19

You cannot buy or bribe your way to salvation and
Heaven. You must humble yourself before Jesus. Only
He can pay the price for your sins.

And thou say in thine heart, My power and the might
of mine hand hath gotten me this wealth.
Deuteronomy 8:17

Pride and ego can be some of our biggest obstacles. Don't let it come between you and the Lord. Remember that every good and perfect gift comes from above.

Neither their silver nor their gold shall be able to deliver them in the day of the LORD's wrath; but the whole land shall be devoured by the fire of his jealousy: for he shall make even a speedy riddance of all them that dwell in the land. Zephaniah 1:18

You can't buy or bribe the Lord. He knows your heart. The only way to honor Him is to humble yourself before Him and obey Him. Ask the Lord to take control of your life.

Brethren, if a man be overtaken in a fault, ye which are spiritual, restore such an one in the spirit of meekness; considering thyself, lest thou also be tempted. Galatians 6:1

Humble, godly suggestions may save a friend from destroying his life. Be a true friend. Live for Jesus and help others know the joy of serving Him.

*And all this assembly shall know that the LORD
saveth not with sword and spear: for the battle is the
LORD's, and he will give you into our hands.*
1 Samuel 17:47

What a wonderful promise. You're not alone. God
will help you. Humble yourself before Him and let
Him show Himself to be mighty in your circumstances.

*Let nothing be done through strife or vainglory; but
in lowliness of mind let each esteem other better
than themselves. Philippians 2:3*

Whatever happened to old-fashioned humility? Let's
consider others before ourselves. That's the way of
Jesus.

*Humble yourselves therefore under the mighty hand
of God, that he may exalt you in due time:
1 Peter 5:6*

Genuine humility is a blessing to God, others, and
yourself. Humble yourself before the Lord and you
can be a blessing and receive a blessing.

Humility—179

So likewise ye, when ye shall have done all those things which are commanded you, say, We are unprofitable servants: we have done that which was our duty to do. Luke 17:10

Humility is a key in serving God and others. Don't complain when you serve. Do it with joy and humility. It makes all the difference in the world.

Verily I say unto you, Whosoever shall not receive the kingdom of God as a little child shall in no wise enter therein. Luke 18:17

Children have great faith. That's why we must come to Jesus like a child. Humble yourself before Him and allow Him to be Lord of your life.

But they refused to hearken, and pulled away the shoulder, and stopped their ears, that they should not hear. Zechariah 7:11

Don't resist the will of God. Stubbornness can be such a hindrance. Let go and let God have His wonderful way.

A man's pride shall bring him low: but honour shall uphold the humble in spirit. Proverbs 29:23

Pride is one of man's worst enemies. If you humble yourself before the Lord and others, you will be a blessing and receive a blessing.

The transgression of the wicked saith within my heart, that there is no fear of God before his eyes. For he flattereth himself in his own eyes, until his iniquity be found to be hateful. Psalm 36:1-2

If you think you're really something, you probably aren't. Humble yourself and let Him get you in touch with reality.

He hath put down the mighty from their seats, and exalted them of low degree. Luke 1:52

God has the final say-so to greatness. Humble yourself before the Lord and He will exalt you. Be His servant and a servant to others and you will know this to be true.

And whosoever shall exalt himself shall be abased;
and he that shall humble himself shall be exalted.
Matthew 23:12

God is the best bookkeeper in the universe. He will
exalt the humble and humble the self-exalted.

And Jesus called a little child unto him, and set him
in the midst of them, And said, Verily I say unto you,
Except ye be converted, and become as little
children, ye shall not enter into the kingdom of
heaven. Matthew 18:2-3

Have you humbled yourself before the Lord and asked
His forgiveness? Faith and humility are essentials for
the child of God.

The wicked, through the pride of his countenance,
will not seek after God: God is not in all his
thoughts. Psalm 10:4

Pride is a tremendous barrier to God. Humble yourself
and seek the Lord. That's the only way we can con-
nect with Him.

Whereupon the princes of Israel and the king humbled themselves; and they said, The LORD is righteous. 2 Chronicles 12:6

Oh that more leaders would humble themselves before the Lord and seek His wisdom and righteousness. Let's pray for our leaders of our land.

Before destruction the heart of man is haughty, and before honour is humility. Proverbs 18:12

Pride leads to destruction. Humility leads to honor. The choice is ours to make.

Wherefore let him that thinketh he standeth take heed lest he fall. 1 Corinthians 10:12

Pride can be our worst enemy. Humble yourself before the Lord.

I came not to call the righteous, but sinners to repentance. Luke 5:32

The Lord cannot save those who do not realize they are sinners. Truly, pride in self is one of the great stumbling blocks to salvation.

If thou, LORD, shouldest mark iniquities, O Lord, who shall stand? But there is forgiveness with thee, that thou mayest be feared. Psalm 130:3-4

I am so grateful that God forgives us of sins when we confess them. He is willing and able if we will humble ourselves in confession.

Verily I say unto you, Whosoever shall not receive the kingdom of God as a little child, he shall not enter therein. Mark 10:15

The humility and trust of a child is needed to enter the Kingdom of God.

The sacrifices of God are a broken spirit: a broken and a contrite heart, O God, thou wilt not despise.
Psalm 51:17

The Lord is interested in our sincere devotion. Let's remain humble before the Lord.

Woe unto them that are wise in their own eyes, and prudent in their own sight! Isaiah 5:21

Pride can blind us as nothing else.

If any of you lack wisdom, let him ask of God, that giveth to all men liberally, and upbraideth not; and it shall be given him. James 1:5

The Lord will give us the wisdom we need. We just need to humble ourselves and ask.

Parents, Husbands, Wives

There was in the days of Herod, the king of Judaea, a certain priest named Zacharias, of the course of Abia: and his wife was of the daughters of Aaron, and her name was Elisabeth. And they were both righteous before God, walking in all the commandments and ordinances of the Lord blameless. Luke 1:5-6

Our world is in desperate need of godly parents. Mom and Dad, are you living for the Lord? Remember, someone is looking at your examples.

Foolishness is bound in the heart of a child; but the rod of correction shall drive it far from him.
Proverbs 22:15

Children cannot rear themselves. Mom and Dad, fulfill your responsibility. Show them the difference between right and wrong in an atmosphere of love.

Correct thy son, and he shall give thee rest; yea, he shall give delight unto thy soul. Proverbs 29:17

Discipline is an act of love. Correct your children with a spirit of love.

And also all that generation were gathered unto their fathers: and there arose another generation after them, which knew not the LORD, nor yet the works which he had done for Israel. Judges 2:10

We are always just one generation away from being totally pagan. Teach your children about the love, power, forgiveness and justice of the Lord. Our children walking with God are the hope for the future.

And Isaac digged again the wells of water, which they had digged in the days of Abraham his father;

for the Philistines had stopped them after the death of Abraham: and he called their names after the names by which his father had called them.
Genesis 26:18

We need to go back to our forefathers' deep roots of faith as Isaac went back to his father's well.

Marriage is honourable in all, and the bed undefiled: but whoremongers and adulterers God will judge. Hebrews 13:4

Our society would do well to remember this exhortation from the Word of God. Love and fidelity are essential to having healthy homes.

He saith unto them, Moses because of the hardness of your hearts suffered you to put away your wives: but from the beginning it was not so. Matthew 19:8

It's time we recognize the devastation of divorce on society. Let's allow Jesus' love to fill our homes. This will make marriage happy and lasting.

There is a generation that curseth their father, and doth not bless their mother. Proverbs 30:11

I'm afraid we live in such a generation. Parents, it's our own fault. We must teach our children respect for authority.

And he did evil in the sight of the LORD, and walked in the way of his father, and in the way of his mother, and in the way of Jeroboam the son of Nebat, who made Israel to sin. 1 Kings 22:52

Parents, we must realize that our children will follow our habits, both good and bad. What kind of example are you?

Let the righteous smite me; it shall be a kindness: and let him reprove me; it shall be an excellent oil, which shall not break my head: for yet my prayer also shall be in their calamities. Psalm 141:5

Correction and direction given to us by the righteous is a wonderful blessing. Listen carefully to what they say.

Husbands, love your wives, and be not bitter against them. Colossians 3:19

Kindness and respect can make a marriage a beautiful sight to behold. Be kind and tender to the one God has given to you as your spouse.

For this child I prayed; and the LORD hath given me my petition which I asked of him: Therefore also I have lent him to the LORD; as long as he liveth he shall be lent to the LORD. And he worshipped the LORD there. 1 Samuel 1:27-28

Have you dedicated your life and the lives of your children to the Lord? It's the greatest thing you can do for yourself and for them.

What therefore God hath joined together, let not man put asunder. Mark 10:9

Commitment is needed for a marriage to work. Are you having trouble? Turn to the Lord for the help you need.

He that spareth his rod hateth his son: but he that loveth him chasteneth him betimes. Proverbs 13:24

Here's the question for every parent to ponder. Do you really love your children? If so, you will discipline them. To fail to do so is to indicate that you do not want to be bothered. Think it over.

When I call to remembrance the unfeigned faith that is in thee, which dwelt first in thy grandmother Lois, and thy mother Eunice; and I am persuaded that in thee also. 2 Timothy 1:5

Parents and, yes, grandparents have the wonderful privilege of passing the faith on to their children and grandchildren. Are we giving our children the opportunity to accept the Lord into their hearts? Read the Bible, pray, and take your children to church.

For this cause shall a man leave his father and mother, and cleave to his wife; And they twain shall be one flesh: so then they are no more twain, but one flesh. What therefore God hath joined together, let not man put asunder. Mark 10:7-9

There have been too many broken homes and broken hearts. We need to get back to the teachings of the Bible. He has the best plan.

Seeing that Abraham shall surely become a great and mighty nation, and all the nations of the earth shall be blessed in him? For I know him, that he will command his children and his household after him, and they shall keep the way of the LORD, to do justice and judgment; that the LORD may bring upon Abraham that which he hath spoken of him.
Genesis 18:18-19

Faith in the Lord must be real at home first. Don't neglect your family.

But Jesus said, Suffer little children, and forbid them not, to come unto me: for of such is the kingdom of heaven. And he laid his hands on them, and departed thence. Matthew 19:14-15

Parents, are you bringing your children to the Lord or are you standing in their way? Jesus longs to bless children.

Thou shalt rise up before the hoary head, and honour the face of the old man, and fear thy God: I am the LORD. Leviticus 19:32

Whatever happened to respect and good manners? Less TV and more Bible would help remedy a great deal of this lack in our society.

We have heard with our ears, O God, our fathers have told us, what work thou didst in their days, in the times of old. Psalm 44:1

Dad, are you taking time to tell your children about the Lord? It's one of the most important items you will share with them.

Withhold not correction from the child: for if thou beatest him with the rod, he shall not die. Thou shalt beat him with the rod, and shalt deliver his soul from hell. Proverbs 23:13-14

Discipline takes love and time. Parents, will we give our children our undivided attention?

Children, obey your parents in the Lord: for this is right. Honour thy father and mother; which is the first commandment with promise; Ephesians 6:1-2

If the family is to survive, we must go back to the basics! This is one of the most important basics of family life.

And said, For this cause shall a man leave father and mother, and shall cleave to his wife: and they twain shall be one flesh? Wherefore they are no more twain, but one flesh. What therefore God hath joined together, let not man put asunder. Matthew 19:5-6

This is still God's plan for marriage. The Lord knows what is best for us. We must get back to following his ways.

Train up a child in the way he should go: and when he is old, he will not depart from it. Proverbs 22:6

Parent, are you taking the time to train your child in the ways of God? If not, you need to readjust your schedule now.

I made a covenant with mine eyes; why then should I think upon a maid? Job 31:1

What wholesome wisdom this is for all men. Devote your heart completely to the wife God has given you. Ask the Lord to help you keep such a covenant.

House and riches are the inheritance of fathers: and a prudent wife is from the LORD. Proverbs 19:14

Husband, when was the last time you expressed appreciation for your wife? Let her know that you love her.

He that spareth his rod hateth his son: but he that loveth him chasteneth him betimes. Proverbs 13:24

Discipline is a sign of love. Parents, be consistent and discipline your children with love.

And thou, Solomon my son, know thou the God of thy father, and serve him with a perfect heart and

with a willing mind: for the LORD searcheth all hearts, and understandeth all the imaginations of the thoughts: if thou seek him, he will be found of thee; but if thou forsake him, he will cast thee off for ever.
1 Chronicles 28:9

We need more father-to-son talks like this in our day.

Foolishness is bound in the heart of a child; but the rod of correction shall drive it far from him.
Proverbs 22:15

It's time we got back to loving discipline in our society. Parents, take the time to guide your children. They are depending on us.

And Ruth said, Intreat me not to leave thee, or to return from following after thee: for whither thou goest, I will go; and where thou lodgest, I will lodge: thy people shall be my people, and thy God my God.
Ruth 1:16

We need more love and loyalty in our lives today. A good place to begin is at home. Take time to love your family.

Correct thy son, and he shall give thee rest; yea, he shall give delight unto thy soul. Proverbs 29:17

Discipline is first learned in the home. Parents, you have a heavy responsibility. Take time to love and discipline your children.

When I call to remembrance the unfeigned faith that is in thee, which dwelt first in thy grandmother Lois, and thy mother Eunice; and I am persuaded that in thee also. 2 Timothy 1:5

The best gift a parent or grandparent can give to a child is a godly heritage. What are you giving your children?

And they brought young children to him, that he should touch them: and his disciples rebuked those that brought them. But when Jesus saw it, he was much displeased, and said unto them, Suffer the little children to come unto me, and forbid them not: for of such is the kingdom of God. Mark 10:13-14

Keeping a child away from Jesus is a major offense in the eyes of God.

But whoso shall offend one of these little ones which believe in me, it were better for him that a millstone were hanged about his neck, and that he were drowned in the depth of the sea. Matthew 18:6

If you've hindered a child from coming to Jesus, watch it. You'll have to deal with God about it.

Likewise greet the church that is in their house. Salute my wellbeloved Epaenetus, who is the firstfruits of Achaia unto Christ. Romans 16:5

There is no substitute for honoring God in our homes. Don't leave Jesus at the church building. Take Him home.

*Likewise, ye husbands, dwell with them according to knowledge, giving honour unto the wife, as unto the weaker vessel, and as being heirs together of the grace of life; that your prayers be not hindered.
1 Peter 3:7*

Our world needs loving, compassionate, tender and praying husbands. Will you be one?

Nevertheless let every one of you in particular so love his wife even as himself; and the wife see that she reverence her husband. Ephesians 5:33

A lot of marriages could come a long way if we just followed this one verse. Husbands, love your wives. Wives, love your husbands with respect.

Whosoever putteth away his wife, and marrieth another, committeth adultery: and whosoever marrieth her that is put away from her husband committeth adultery. Luke 16:18

Divorce is not the answer to marital strife. Let Jesus' love take full control and see how He can heal a broken relationship.

But Jesus called them unto him, and said, Suffer little children to come unto me, and forbid them not: for of such is the kingdom of God. Luke 18:16

Let's give our children the opportunity to come to Jesus. Make sure that you and your children are in a Bible-teaching church.

Peace

*Let us walk honestly, as in the day; not in rioting
and drunkenness, not in chambering and
wantonness, not in strife and envying. But put ye
on the Lord Jesus Christ, and make not provision
for the flesh, to fulfil the lusts thereof.*
Romans 13:13-14

In this day of materialism and greed we have forgotten to make provision for the soul. Only Jesus can bring peace to the human heart. "Put on the Lord Jesus Christ."

*And he shall judge among the nations, and shall
rebuke many people: and they shall beat their
swords into plowshares, and their spears into
pruninghooks: nation shall not lift up sword against
nation, neither shall they learn war any more.*
Isaiah 2:4

Only the Lord Himself can bring real peace to individuals and nations. Let Him give you the peace that passes all understanding. Crown Him Lord of your life.

Better is little with the fear of the LORD than great treasure and trouble therewith. Proverbs 15:16

Peace of mind is much more valuable than material wealth. The Lord is One who can give you that peace.

And Paul, earnestly beholding the council, said, Men and brethren, I have lived in all good conscience before God until this day. Acts 23:1

There's only one way to have this kind of peace. A person must surrender himself to the Lord. Will you be that kind of person?

*I will both lay me down in peace, and sleep: for thou, LORD, only makest me dwell in safety.
Psalm 4:8*

Are rest and sleep hard to find? Put your trust in the Lord and experience His wonderful peace.

Peace I leave with you, my peace I give unto you: not as the world giveth, give I unto you. Let not your heart be troubled, neither let it be afraid.
John 14:27

You can have real peace. Place your life and your cares into the hands of Jesus.

And Jesus came and touched them, and said, Arise, and be not afraid. Matthew 17:7

Jesus will touch your life with peace if you will let Him. He can calm the storms of your life. Give your burden to Him.

And the LORD spake unto Moses, saying, Phinehas, the son of Eleazar, the son of Aaron the priest, hath turned my wrath away from the children of Israel, while he was zealous for my sake among them, that I

consumed not the children of Israel in my jealousy.
Wherefore say, Behold, I give unto him my covenant
of peace. Numbers 25:10-12

Don't be halfhearted for the Lord. Give Him your heart and experience His peace.

Teach me thy way, O LORD; I will walk in thy truth:
unite my heart to fear thy name. Psalm 86:11

Frustration comes to a child of God when he has a divided heart. Walk wholeheartedly in God's truth and find peace instead of frustration.

I waited patiently for the LORD; and he inclined unto
me, and heard my cry. He brought me up also out of
an horrible pit, out of the miry clay, and set my feet
upon a rock, and established my goings.
Psalm 40:1-2

Walking with the Lord can bring peace and stability to your life. Look to Him. Trust Him.

Thou wilt keep him in perfect peace, whose mind is stayed on thee: because he trusteth in thee.
Isaiah 26:3

Do you want peace of mind? Keep your thoughts on the Lord. He has everything under control.

And he said, Come. And when Peter was come down out of the ship, he walked on the water, to go to Jesus. But when he saw the wind boisterous, he was afraid; and beginning to sink, he cried, saying, Lord, save me. Matthew 14:29-30

Jesus is still in the saving business. If you're drowning in grief, fear, depression, and doubt, turn to Jesus. He will lift you out of the waves of despair.

The LORD is nigh unto them that are of a broken heart; and saveth such as be of a contrite spirit. Many are the afflictions of the righteous: but the LORD delivereth him out of them all.
Psalm 34:18-19

The Lord will see you through your crisis. Lean on Him for peace and strength.

God is our refuge and strength, a very present help in trouble. Therefore will not we fear, though the earth be removed, and though the mountains be carried into the midst of the sea. Psalm 46:1-2

The Lord gives great peace and confidence when we are depending on Him. Cast your burdens on the Lord. He loves you.

The sleep of a labouring man is sweet, whether he eat little or much: but the abundance of the rich will not suffer him to sleep. Ecclesiastes 5:12

Work is to be enjoyed. It can bring peace to the heart. Hoarding wealth, on the other hand, brings many a sleepless night.

It is vain for you to rise up early, to sit up late, to eat the bread of sorrows: for so he giveth his beloved sleep. Psalm 127:2

Sleep comes easier when we know that we are secure in the loving arms of God. Do you have that kind of peace? It's a wonderful blessing.

He healeth the broken in heart, and bindeth up their wounds. Psalm 147:3

The Lord can heal the wounds of your life too. Give your burdens to the Lord.

But godliness with contentment is great gain. For we brought nothing into this world, and it is certain we can carry nothing out. 1 Timothy 6:6-7

This puts life and things into clear perspective. Walk with God and experience peace.

And he said unto her, Daughter, thy faith hath made thee whole; go in peace, and be whole of thy plague. Mark 5:34

Jesus can bring wholeness and peace to our lives too, if we will place our faith in Him.

I will not leave you comfortless: I will come to you. John 14:18

When you trust in Jesus you are never alone.

Thus saith the LORD, thy Redeemer, the Holy One of Israel; I am the LORD thy God which teacheth thee to profit, which leadeth thee by the way that thou shouldest go. O that thou hadst hearkened to my commandments! then had thy peace been as a river, and thy righteousness as the waves of the sea.
Isaiah 48:17-18

The reason we lack the peace of God is because we fail to listen to Him. Take time to let God speak to you through the Bible.

But the salvation of the righteous is of the LORD: he is their strength in the time of trouble. Psalm 37:39

The Lord is always present for His people. Let Him be your strength in the time of trouble.

The righteous cry, and the LORD heareth, and delivereth them out of all their troubles. The LORD

*is nigh unto them that are of a broken heart; and
saveth such as be of a contrite spirit.
Psalm 34:17-18*

Sometimes life hurts. Cry out to the Lord and let Him bring peace to your life. He loves you.

What shall we then say to these things? If God be for us, who can be against us? Romans 8:31

Walking with God surely brings confidence. Do you have that peace and assurance? You can by trusting Jesus with all the details of your life.

*Be careful for nothing; but in every thing by prayer and supplication with thanksgiving let your requests be made known unto God. And the peace of God, which passeth all understanding, shall keep your hearts and minds through Christ Jesus.
Philippians 4:6-7*

Jesus will give you peace in the midst of the storms of life. Call on Him with your needs.

He that covereth his sins shall not prosper: but whoso confesseth and forsaketh them shall have mercy. Proverbs 28:13

Attempting to cover up your sin will not give you peace. Confess them to the Lord and forsake them. This is where real joy can be found.

For his anger endureth but a moment; in his favour is life: weeping may endure for a night, but joy cometh in the morning. Psalm 30:5

Those tears won't last forever. Joy comes in the morning. Let the Lord bring healing to your broken heart.

Therefore being justified by faith, we have peace with God through our Lord Jesus Christ: Romans 5:1

Christians have peace within because they have Jesus in their hearts. It's wonderful to be a Christian.

What time I am afraid, I will trust in thee.
Psalm 56:3

Peace can come in the midst of uncertainty when we put our trust in God. Have faith in God.

I laid me down and slept; I awaked; for the LORD sustained me. Psalm 3:5

You can rest well when you know the Lord is with you. He is the One who gives us the peace that passes all understanding.

The LORD will give strength unto his people; the LORD will bless his people with peace. Psalm 29:11

The Lord will give you the strength and peace you need. He loves you.

And let the peace of God rule in your hearts, to the which also ye are called in one body; and be ye thankful. Colossians 3:15

Think on Jesus and watch His peace replace your anx iety.

For I have satiated the weary soul, and I have replenished every sorrowful soul. Jeremiah 31:25

The Lord will bring refreshing to your soul also if you will cast your care upon Him. Give that burden to the Lord.

Follow peace with all men, and holiness, without which no man shall see the Lord: Hebrews 12:14

God's holiness and peace within us will allow others to see Jesus in us. Be a witness for Jesus.

In the multitude of my thoughts within me thy comforts delight my soul. Psalm 94:19

Replace the anxieties of your life with the blessed peace of the Lord. Draw close to the Lord and let His peace reign within your heart.

Come unto me, all ye that labour and are heavy laden, and I will give you rest. Matthew 11:28

Unload your cares upon the Lord. He will give you the peace for which you so desperately long.

These things I have spoken unto you, that in me ye might have peace. In the world ye shall have tribulation: but be of good cheer; I have overcome the world. John 16:33

Life has its problems and Jesus has the answers to those problems. Let Him give you peace and victory in all your situations.

For godly sorrow worketh repentance to salvation not to be repented of: but the sorrow of the world worketh death. 2 Corinthians 7:10

Godly sorrow brings forth a new life. Just feeling sorry brings no peace. Turn your cares and failures over to the Lord and let Him give you new life.

Then the same day at evening, being the first day of the week, when the doors were shut where the disciples were assembled for fear of the Jews, came Jesus and stood in the midst, and saith unto them, Peace be unto you. John 20:19

Don't be afraid. Jesus stands ready to speak to your heart and soul. He loves you!

And he saith unto them, Why are ye fearful, O ye of little faith? Then he arose, and rebuked the winds and the sea; and there was a great calm.
Matthew 8:26

Jesus can still the storms of your life too. Have faith in Him. He can give you the peace that passes all understanding.

For God is not the author of confusion, but of peace, as in all churches of the saints. 1 Corinthians 14:33

Are you looking for God's will? Follow the road that leads to peace and reject the one that leads to confusion.

Peace I leave with you, my peace I give unto you: not as the world giveth, give I unto you. Let not your heart be troubled, neither let it be afraid.
John 14:27

No one or nothing can give you peace like Jesus. Don't be afraid to face life. Surrender your circumstances to Jesus.

I have fought a good fight, I have finished my course, I have kept the faith. 2 Timothy 4:7

There is great peace to those who walk with God. Paul had that peace and assurance. How about you?

But let every man prove his own work, and then shall he have rejoicing in himself alone, and not in another. Galatians 6:4

Self worth does not come to us by comparing ourselves to others. It comes to us by being at peace with God and by making the most of what God has given you. Let the Lord lead you and see what He can do through you.

*For where envying and strife is, there is confusion
and every evil work. James 3:16*

There is a lot to be said for being at peace with God
and with others. Avoid argument. Seek to be a healer
and not a hurter.

*Let us not be desirous of vain glory, provoking one
another, envying one another. Galatians 5:26*

Contentment sure beats jealousy. Jesus can give you
that peace of mind. Get rid of the stress in your life.
Give your life to Him.

*But now in Christ Jesus ye who sometimes were far
off are made nigh by the blood of Christ. For he is
our peace, who hath made both one, and hath
broken down the middle wall of partition between us.
Ephesians 2:13-14*

The peace you so desperately long for will not be
yours until you come to know the Prince of Peace.
You've tried everything else. Trust Jesus and see what
He can do.

Now no chastening for the present seemeth to be joyous, but grievous: nevertheless afterward it yieldeth the peaceable fruit of righteousness unto them which are exercised thereby. Hebrews 12:11

God disciplines us because He loves us. Be patient. God is up to something special in your life. In time, His discipline will bring us peace.

Jesus answered and said unto him, If a man love me, he will keep my words: and my Father will love him, and we will come unto him, and make our abode with him. John 14:23

Loving Jesus means that we will obey Him. It also means that our heart becomes His home. Let Jesus warm the fires of your heart with love, peace, and joy.

Prayer

And for this cause God shall send them strong delusion, that they should believe a lie: That they all might be damned who believed not the truth, but had pleasure in unrighteousness.
2 Thessalonians 2:11-12

The consequences of sin and unbelief are horrible. People so want to sin and believe the lies of Satan that God gives them up to their own deceits. Pray that societies will be awakened out of their spiritual slumber.

Peter therefore was kept in prison: but prayer was made without ceasing of the church unto God for him. Acts 12:5

It's great to be a part of a church that is concerned about you. Just think. Someone may be praying for you right now. You're not alone. God and others care.

*And he withdrew himself into the wilderness, and
prayed. Luke 5:16*

If Jesus had to withdraw from the activities of the day
to pray, what about us? Take time to pray. It's important.

*Wrath is cruel, and anger is outrageous; but who is
able to stand before envy? Proverbs 27:4*

Is jealousy eating you alive? Start praying for the person of whom you are envious and see the change God
can bring to your attitude.

*As the hart panteth after the water brooks, so
panteth my soul after thee, O God. My soul thirsteth
for God, for the living God: when shall I come and
appear before God? Psalm 42:1-2*

Do you feel like the psalmist? The Lord will come to
you too. "Call unto me, and I will answer thee, and
shew thee great and mighty things, which thou knowest not." (Jeremiah 33:3)

For whosoever shall call upon the name of the Lord
shall be saved. Romans 10:13

You are only a prayer away from joy and fulfillment.
Call on Jesus to save you from your sin. Make Him
Lord of your life.

Watch ye and pray, lest ye enter into temptation. The
spirit truly is ready, but the flesh is weak.
Mark 14:38

Prayer sharpens the spiritual sensitivity of Christians.
It helps us to realize that spiritual growth must have
priority in our lives. Take time to pray.

I love the LORD, because he hath heard my voice
and my supplications. Because he hath inclined his
ear unto me, therefore will I call upon him as
long as I live. Psalm 116:1-2

There is Someone who always has a listening ear. Tell
Him all about it. He loves you.

And he arose, and rebuked the wind, and said unto the sea, Peace, be still. And the wind ceased, and there was a great calm. Mark 4:39

There is a cure for worry and stress. His name is Jesus. Let Him bring a great calm into your life. Pray and share your burden with Him.

And he taught, saying unto them, Is it not written, My house shall be called of all nations the house of prayer? but ye have made it a den of thieves. Mark 11:17

How much praying are we doing in God's house and in our homes? Could this be the one vital ingredient missing in our world today?

The effectual fervent prayer of a righteous man availeth much. James 5:16b

The sincere prayer of a righteous man can make a great difference. This righteousness is found only in Jesus. Give your heart to Him and be a real prayer warrior.

And all the king's servants, that were in the king's gate, bowed, and reverenced Haman: for the king had so commanded concerning him. But Mordecai bowed not, nor did him reverence. Esther 3:2

Lord, give us people who will not bow the knee to evil and evil men. Help us to stand up and be counted for you no matter what the cost. Thank you for hearing our prayer.

I thank God, whom I serve from my forefathers with pure conscience, that without ceasing I have remembrance of thee in my prayers night and day. 2 Timothy 1:3

There must really be something to prayer if the apostle Paul prayed for Timothy both day and night. I wonder who could use your prayer for them right now?

And he said unto them, Come ye yourselves apart into a desert place, and rest a while: for there were many coming and going, and they had no leisure so much as to eat. Mark 6:31

Sometimes we must simply drop our activities and get alone with Jesus. Is it time for you to refill your cup in the presence of the Lord?

Continue in prayer, and watch in the same with thanksgiving. Colossians 4:2

Christian, are you praying? It's important. It may be the most important work we do in our walk with the Lord. "Continue in prayer."

He that planted the ear, shall he not hear? he that formed the eye, shall he not see? Psalm 94:9

God can hear you when you pray. He can see the needs of your life. He is able to help you. Pray to Him now. He loves you.

But your iniquities have separated between you and your God, and your sins have hid his face from you, that he will not hear. Isaiah 59:2

Are you having trouble with your prayer life? Could it be that sin is standing in the way?

And in the morning, rising up a great while before day, he went out, and departed into a solitary place, and there prayed. Mark 1:35

If prayer was that important to Jesus, it should be that important to us.

And said unto them, Why sleep ye? rise and pray, lest ye enter into temptation. Luke 22:46

We cannot afford to be asleep spiritually or morally in these changing times. We must pray. Keep your eyes on Jesus.

Shew me thy ways, O LORD; teach me thy paths. Psalm 25:4

More prayers like this would sure spare us a lot of grief. Let's seek the Lord with all our hearts.

Saying unto them, It is written, My house is the house of prayer: but ye have made it a den of thieves. Luke 19:46

Are we spending enough time in prayer at home and at church? We are told to pray without ceasing.

Moreover as for me, God forbid that I should sin against the LORD in ceasing to pray for you: but I will teach you the good and the right way.
1 Samuel 12:23

Prayerlessness is sin. Let's be a praying people. More than anything else, people need our sincere prayer for them.

Likewise the Spirit also helpeth our infirmities: for we know not what we should pray for as we ought: but the Spirit itself maketh intercession for us with groanings which cannot be uttered. Romans 8:26

Sometimes words can't describe the pain we feel. Get on your knees and pour your heart out to God. He understands.

Then Peter and the other apostles answered and said, We ought to obey God rather than men.
Acts 5:29

Oh how we have a need for such commitment to God today. Lord give us people who love you more than the things of this world.

Behold, the LORD's hand is not shortened, that it cannot save; neither his ear heavy, that it cannot hear: But your iniquities have separated between you and your God, and your sins have hid his face from you, that he will not hear. Isaiah 59:1-2

God can and will answer prayer. Our job is to make sure that our unconfessed sin does not stand in the way of His working in our lives.

Watch and pray, that ye enter not into temptation: the spirit indeed is willing, but the flesh is weak.
Matthew 26:41

Watchful prayer is a tremendous asset in our walk with God. Are we taking time to do it?

Help, LORD; for the godly man ceaseth; for the
faithful fail from among the children of men.
Psalm 12:1

This prayer could certainly be echoed today. The Lord is eager to raise up people who will count for Him. Will you be one?

There are many devices in a man's heart;
nevertheless the counsel of the LORD, that shall
stand. Proverbs 19:21

When you make plans make sure you check with the Lord. A sign on my desk says it best: "Have you prayed about it?"

But when ye pray, use not vain repetitions, as the
heathen do: for they think that they shall be heard
for their much speaking. Be not ye therefore like unto
them: for your Father knoweth what things ye have
need of, before ye ask him. Matthew 6:7-8

We serve a great and compassionate God. He wants to meet your needs. Share those needs and wait on the Lord.

The righteous cry, and the LORD heareth, and
delivereth them out of all their troubles.
Psalm 34:17

Cry out to God. He hears and He delivers His people.

The LORD is on my side; I will not fear: what can
man do unto me? Psalm 118:6

Walking with God brings great confidence. "Take time to be holy. Speak often with the Lord."

O thou that hearest prayer, unto thee shall all flesh
come. Psalm 65:2

God is waiting to hear from you. Drop to your knees and tell Him the burdens of your heart.

And the LORD turned the captivity of Job, when he
prayed for his friends: also the LORD gave Job twice
as much as he had before. Job 42:10

God will take care of us if we are careful to pray for the needs of others.

Even the youths shall faint and be weary, and the young men shall utterly fall: But they that wait upon the LORD shall renew their strength; they shall mount up with wings as eagles; they shall run, and not be weary; and they shall walk, and not faint.
Isaiah 40:30-31

The Lord will give you the boost you need. Call on Him now.

If I regard iniquity in my heart, the Lord will not hear me. Psalm 66:18

Sin stands in the way of a powerful prayer life. Claim 1 John 1:9. "If we confess our sins, he is faithful and just to forgive us our sins, and to cleanse us from all unrighteousness." Now watch God work in your prayer life.

But thou, when thou prayest, enter into thy closet, and when thou hast shut thy door, pray to thy Father which is in secret; and thy Father which seeth in secret shall reward thee openly. Matthew 6:6

When was the last time you went to God in genuine prayer? Take advantage of this wonderful opportunity.

Let the words of my mouth, and the meditation of my heart, be acceptable in thy sight, O LORD, my strength, and my redeemer. Psalm 19:14

May this be our prayer today and everyday. What a wonderful world we can make if we will just live by these words.

I waited patiently for the LORD; and he inclined unto me, and heard my cry. He brought me up also out of an horrible pit, out of the miry clay, and set my feet upon a rock, and established my goings.
Psalm 40:1-2

The Lord will come to you too, if you cry out to Him. He loves you.

*Count not thine handmaid for a daughter of Belial:
for out of the abundance of my complaint and grief
have I spoken hitherto. 1 Samuel 1:16*

When was the last time you prayed with a broken
heart?

*Now the God of patience and consolation grant you
to be likeminded one toward another according to
Christ Jesus: That ye may with one mind and one
mouth glorify God, even the Father of our Lord
Jesus Christ. Romans 15:5-6*

May the people of the Lord Jesus pray this prayer.
Let's praise the Lord with our lives, love, and service.

*LORD, make me to know mine end, and the measure
of my days, what it is; that I may know how frail I
am. Behold, thou hast made my days as an
handbreadth; and mine age is as nothing before
thee: verily every man at his best state is altogether
vanity. Selah. Psalm 39:4-5*

This daily prayer will certainly put life into perspective.

I sought the LORD, and he heard me, and delivered me from all my fears. Psalm 34:4

God answers prayer. Share the burdens of your heart with Him. He loves you.

O LORD, though our iniquities testify against us, do thou it for thy name's sake: for our backslidings are many; we have sinned against thee. Jeremiah 14:7

We need this same kind of revival praying today. May God have mercy on our land.

Set a watch, O LORD, before my mouth; keep the door of my lips. Psalm 141:3

This prayer could keep us out of a lot of trouble. May our words be kind and thoughtful.

Ask, and it shall be given you; seek, and ye shall find; knock, and it shall be opened unto you: For every one that asketh receiveth; and he that seeketh

findeth; and to him that knocketh it shall be opened.
Matthew 7:7-8

This is Jesus' invitation to pray. God answers prayer.

Create in me a clean heart, O God; and renew a
right spirit within me. Psalm 51:10

This sincere prayer would do us all good. God is looking for people with hearts that are open to Him.

For we can do nothing against the truth, but for the
truth. 2 Corinthians 13:8

May the Lord give us more men and women of this conviction: "Lord, help us to love the truth."

Teach me thy way, O LORD; I will walk in thy truth:
unite my heart to fear thy name. Psalm 86:11

We would all do well to pray such a prayer every day. It would bless God, others, and ourselves.

And he spake a parable unto them to this end, that men ought always to pray, and not to faint.
Luke 18:1

Prayer makes a difference. Don't give up. God answers prayer.

And when he was at the place, he said unto them, Pray that ye enter not into temptation. Luke 22:40

Prayer is one of the keys to a victorious life in Jesus. Take time to pray.

Now when Daniel knew that the writing was signed, he went into his house; and his windows being open in his chamber toward Jerusalem, he kneeled upon his knees three times a day, and prayed, and gave thanks before his God, as he did aforetime.
Daniel 6:10

What a wonderful world this would be if we stayed on our knees before the Lord like Daniel did. Take time to pray.

$\mathcal{R}$epentance

For the terrible one is brought to nought, and the scorner is consumed, and all that watch for iniquity are cut off. Isaiah 29:20

Serving sin has a pay day. Repent before it is too late. Ask the Lord to save you from the power and consequences of sin.

Woe unto them that seek deep to hide their counsel from the LORD, and their works are in the dark, and they say, Who seeth us? and who knoweth us? Isaiah 29:15

You can't hide your actions from God. Acknowledge your sin and repent of it. The Lord will cleanse you and deliver you from the slavery of sin.

The backslider in heart shall be filled with his own ways: and a good man shall be satisfied from himself. Proverbs 14:14

The worst slavery of all is to be enslaved by one's own selfishness. Let the Lord set you free. Repent of your sin and selfishness and let Him bring a breath of fresh air to your life.

And the children of Israel cried unto the LORD, saying, We have sinned against thee, both because we have forsaken our God, and also served Baalim. Judges 10:10

The first step of getting our hearts right with God is to cry to Him with a genuine heart of repentance. Do you need to rededicate your life to the Lord?

From that time Jesus began to preach, and to say, Repent: for the kingdom of heaven is at hand. Matthew 4:17

We must never forget that in turning to the Lord we by necessity turn our backs to sin. Salvation comes to only repentant hearts.

For the wages of sin is death; but the gift of God is eternal life through Jesus Christ our Lord.
Romans 6:23

You have a choice. You can die in your sins or you can repent of your sins and accept God's gift of salvation. Make the right decision.

Nevertheless I have somewhat against thee, because thou hast left thy first love. Revelation 2:4

Christian, do you love Jesus as much as you used to love Him? If not, repent and ask the Lord to rekindle that love in your heart. Do it now. Time is slipping away.

Or despisest thou the riches of his goodness and forbearance and longsuffering; not knowing that the goodness of God leadeth thee to repentance?
Romans 2:4

Are you aware of how patient and good God has been to you? Do not take it for granted. Let His love lead you to repentance of sin and acceptance of His wonderful salvation.

And men were scorched with great heat, and blasphemed the name of God, which hath power over these plagues: and they repented not to give him glory. Revelation 16:9

God uses judgment to get our attention. It's up to us to repent of our sins and draw close to Him.

And saying, The time is fulfilled, and the kingdom of God is at hand: repent ye, and believe the gospel. Mark 1:15

Remember that repentance (turning away from sin) is a vital part of salvation. Jesus came not to save us in our sins but from our sins.

Therefore say unto the house of Israel, Thus saith the Lord GOD; Repent, and turn yourselves from your idols; and turn away your faces from all your abominations. Ezekiel 14:6

We need this old-fashioned repentance of sin in our day. What needs to be dealt with in your own life? Repent and experience God's forgiveness and cleansing.

*And refused to obey, neither were mindful of thy
wonders that thou didst among them; but hardened
their necks, and in their rebellion appointed a cap-
tain to return to their bondage: but thou art a God
ready to pardon, gracious and merciful, slow
to anger, and of great kindness, and forsookest
them not. Nehemiah 9:17*

The Lord will forgive if we repent. He's waiting on you.

*Now when Ezra had prayed, and when he had
confessed, weeping and casting himself down before
the house of God, there assembled unto him out of
Israel a very great congregation of men and women
and children: for the people wept very sore.
Ezra 10:1*

Oh that we would fall on our faces before God in confession and repentance. God would heal our broken
hearts. He's ready. Are we?

*And David said unto God, I have sinned greatly,
because I have done this thing: but now, I beseech
thee, do away the iniquity of thy servant; for I have
done very foolishly. 1 Chronicles 21:8*

Confession and repentance are necessary steps in getting our hearts right with God. "Come clean" with God and let Him make a wonderful difference in your life.

And I will cleanse them from all their iniquity, whereby they have sinned against me; and I will pardon all their iniquities, whereby they have sinned, and whereby they have transgressed against me. Jeremiah 33:8

If we repent, the Lord will forgive. Let Him bring cleansing and peace to your heart.

But if ye will not drive out the inhabitants of the land from before you; then it shall come to pass, that those which ye let remain of them shall be pricks in your eyes, and thorns in your sides, and shall vex you in the land wherein ye dwell. Numbers 33:55

Are there inhabitants of selfishness, greed, jealousy, coveting, hatred, etc. that need to be driven away? Don't tolerate these. Ask the Lord to help you rid yourself of these enemies.

For godly sorrow worketh repentance to salvation not to be repented of: but the sorrow of the world worketh death. 2 Corinthians 7:10

The regret and sorrow of this world leads to despair and death. There is a better way. Repent of sin and be saved and forgiven.

For Demas hath forsaken me, having loved this present world, and is departed unto Thessalonica; Crescens to Galatia, Titus unto Dalmatia. 2 Timothy 4:10

Are you a spiritual dropout? Repent and serve the Lord with all your heart.

Jesus answered and said unto him, Verily, verily, I say unto thee, Except a man be born again, he cannot see the kingdom of God. John 3:3

You cannot be a child of the Lord unless you've been born again. Repent of sin and ask Jesus to be your Savior and Lord.

*Have I any pleasure at all that the wicked should
die? saith the Lord GOD: and not that he should
return from his ways, and live? Ezekiel 18:23*

The Lord can and wants to forgive the sins of your
past. Repent and let Him be the Lord of your life. He
loves you.

*Son of man, these men have set up their idols in their
heart, and put the stumbling block of their iniquity
before their face: should I be enquired of at all by
them? Ezekiel 14:3*

Idols in our hearts can hinder our walk with God.
Repent and forsake these idols and follow the Lord
with all your heart.

*As the LORD commanded Moses his servant, so did
Moses command Joshua, and so did Joshua; he left
nothing undone of all that the LORD commanded
Moses. Joshua 11:15*

Are we leaving any of God's business undone? If so,
let's repent and follow the example of Moses and
Joshua. Obey the Lord.

Wherefore God also gave them up to uncleanness through the lusts of their own hearts, to dishonour their own bodies between themselves: Romans 1:24

Sin brings its own consequences. One of the worst consequences is that God gives up people to their own lusts. The result is self destruction. Repent and turn to the Lord before it is too late.

And the second time the cock crew. And Peter called to mind the word that Jesus said unto him, Before the cock crow twice, thou shalt deny me thrice. And when he thought thereon, he wept. Mark 14:72

Peter did wrong to deny the Lord, but he had the insight and humility to weep and repent. Our world needs tender hearts like that.

*Woe unto them that call evil good, and good evil; that put darkness for light, and light for darkness; that put bitter for sweet, and sweet for bitter!
Isaiah 5:20*

What a vivid description of our society today. It reads like today's newspaper. By the way, this verse was written 700 years plus before the birth of Christ. Let's repent before we too come under God's judgment.

And the rest of the men which were not killed by these plagues yet repented not of the works of their hands, that they should not worship devils, and idols of gold, and silver, and brass, and stone, and of wood: which neither can see, nor hear, nor walk: Neither repented they of their murders, nor of their sorceries, nor of their fornication, nor of their thefts.
Revelation 9:20-21

Hardening your heart toward God is certain doom. Repent of your sin before it is everlastingly too late.

For I have no pleasure in the death of him that dieth, saith the Lord GOD: wherefore turn yourselves, and live ye. Ezekiel 18:32

The Lord wants you to experience life at its best. To do this we must repent of our sins. Are you willing to repent and live life at its best?

*And Samuel spake unto all the house of Israel,
saying, If ye do return unto the LORD with all your
hearts, then put away the strange gods and
Ashtaroth from among you, and prepare your hearts
unto the LORD, and serve him only: and he will
deliver you out of the hand of the Philistines.*
1 Samuel 7:3

A turning to the Lord necessitates that we must turn
away from sin. Repentance is an important part of our
walk with the Lord.

*Therefore say thou unto them, Thus saith the LORD of
hosts; Turn ye unto me, saith the LORD of hosts, and
I will turn unto you, saith the LORD of hosts.*
Zechariah 1:3

Repentance is one of the keys of getting our hearts in
tune with God. Are you ready to do business with God?

*Sow to yourselves in righteousness, reap in mercy;
break up your fallow ground: for it is time to seek
the LORD, till he come and rain righteousness upon
you. Hosea 10:12*

Is it time for you to seek the Lord? Repent now and throw yourself on the mercy of God.

And they went out, and preached that men should repent. Mark 6:12

The message of confession and repentance is needed now as much as ever. Forgiveness only comes when we genuinely repent.

It is a fearful thing to fall into the hands of the living God. Hebrews 10:31

It is not trivial matter to be judged by God. Repent and be saved by Jesus before it is everlastingly too late.

For they have sown the wind, and they shall reap the whirlwind: it hath no stalk: the bud shall yield no meal: if so be it yield, the strangers shall swallow it up. Hosea 8:7

When you sow the seeds of sin you will reap the whirlwind of its consequences. Repent of sin and follow the Lord. He has a better plan for you.

Nevertheless I have somewhat against thee, because thou hast left thy first love. Remember therefore from whence thou art fallen, and repent, and do the first works; or else I will come unto thee quickly, and will remove thy candlestick out of his place, except thou repent. Revelation 2:4-5

Dear Christian, do you love Jesus as much as you used to love Him? If not, repent and love Him with all your heart.

And they rejected his statutes, and his covenant that he made with their fathers, and his testimonies which he testified against them; and they followed vanity, and became vain, and went after the heathen that were round about them, concerning whom the LORD had charged them, that they should not do like them. 2 Kings 17:15

Do you have a rebellious spirit toward God? Repent. Love and serve the Lord. He loves you.

For my thoughts are not your thoughts, neither are your ways my ways, saith the LORD. For as the heavens are higher than the earth, so are my ways higher than your ways, and my thoughts than your thoughts. Isaiah 55:8-9

The Lord will forgive if we repent. Take God at His Word today.

But he, being full of compassion, forgave their iniquity, and destroyed them not: yea, many a time turned he his anger away, and did not stir up all his wrath. Psalm 78:38

The Lord is more than willing to forgive if we will just repent of sin.

Now after that John was put in prison, Jesus came into Galilee, preaching the gospel of the kingdom of God, And saying, The time is fulfilled, and the kingdom of God is at hand: repent ye, and believe the gospel. Mark 1:14-15

To experience God's forgiveness we must repent. Repent means to turn away from our sins.

Many times did he deliver them; but they provoked him with their counsel, and were brought low for their iniquity. Psalm 106:43

We can't keep taking God's mercy and patience for granted. Repent and follow Him with all your heart.

Thou hast set our iniquities before thee, our secret sins in the light of thy countenance. Psalm 90:8

You can't hide your sins from God. Repent of your sins and ask God's forgiveness. He loves you.

And he did not many mighty works there because of their unbelief. Matthew 13:58

Is our unbelief quenching God's work? Is so, let's repent and place our total faith in God.

I tell you, Nay: but, except ye repent, ye shall all likewise perish. Luke 13:3

Repent means to turn away from our sins and to turn to Jesus and His ways. This is not an option of salvation. It is a must.

Against thee, thee only, have I sinned, and done this evil in thy sight: that thou mightest be justified when thou speakest, and be clear when thou judgest.
Psalm 51:4

Remember, all sin is against God. There are no acceptable excuses. We must repent.

He that covereth his sins shall not prosper: but whoso confesseth and forsaketh them shall have mercy. Proverbs 28:13

Cover-up of our sins brings misery. Confession to God brings mercy. The choice is yours to make.

Revival

For your obedience is come abroad unto all men. I am glad therefore on your behalf: but yet I would have you wise unto that which is good, and simple concerning evil. Romans 16:19

May God have mercy on us so that we may be innocent about what is evil and wise about what is good. Lord, send a revival.

But Peter and John answered and said unto them, Whether it be right in the sight of God to hearken unto you more than unto God, judge ye. For we cannot but speak the things which we have seen and heard. Acts 4:19-20

May God's people overcome with God's presence as these great men of old. We need a spiritual awakening like this in our world.

Having therefore these promises, dearly beloved, let us cleanse ourselves from all filthiness of the flesh and spirit, perfecting holiness in the fear of God.
2 Corinthians 7:1

This is the kind of revival we need today. Let's reject sin and clothe ourselves in God's holiness.

Now when Ezra had prayed, and when he had confessed, weeping and casting himself down before the house of God, there assembled unto him out of Israel a very great congregation of men and women and children: for the people wept very sore.
Ezra 10:1

Should we too be on our knees in deep conviction of sin? This is always where revival begins. Lord, send a revival.

Rivers of waters run down mine eyes, because they keep not thy law. Psalm 119:136

Are our hearts broken because of the sin and immorality that is so prevalent around us? Let us weep and pray for revival.

And they shall teach my people the difference between the holy and profane, and cause them to discern between the unclean and the clean.
Ezekiel 44:23

Our world needs more men who will unapologetically live and teach the truth. Lord, send us a revival.

Because that, when they knew God, they glorified him not as God, neither were thankful; but became vain in their imaginations, and their foolish heart was darkened. Professing themselves to be wise, they became fools. Romans 1:21-22

Unfortunately this sounds like today. Is it no wonder that our world is going crazy? We need to turn back to God.

Ye shall not steal, neither deal falsely, neither lie one to another. Leviticus 19:11

If we would only return to God and His ways we would be so much better. Lord, send a revival of honesty and integrity to our land.

Thou shalt not avenge, nor bear any grudge against the children of thy people, but thou shalt love thy neighbour as thyself: I am the LORD. Leviticus 19:18

We need a revival of respect for the elderly and for God. This would take care of some of the ills of our society.

According to their pasture, so were they filled; they were filled, and their heart was exalted; therefore have they forgotten me. Hosea 13:6

Have we taken God and His goodness for granted? If we have, we are the losers. Let's give God the glory for the way He has provided for us.

Traitors, heady, highminded, lovers of pleasures more than lovers of God. 2 Timothy 3:4

Christians are you more in love with pleasure and comfort than you are in love with Jesus? If so, there is need for revival in your heart.

Why then is this people of Jerusalem slidden back by a perpetual backsliding? they hold fast deceit, they refuse to return. Jeremiah 8:5

Our country needs some old-fashioned repentance of sin. Let's quit offering excuses for our sinfulness and get on with the business of loving and serving the Lord.

Marriage is honourable in all, and the bed undefiled: but whoremongers and adulterers God will judge. Hebrews 13:4

We need a revival of marital fidelity and faithfulness in our world. Sexual immorality is destroying lives and families daily. Lord help us to return to the teachings of the Bible.

The disciple is not above his master, nor the servant above his lord. Matthew 10:24

We need a revival of respect of authority. This is especially true when it comes to Christians obeying the Lord. Remember, He is in charge.

And because iniquity shall abound, the love of many shall wax cold. Matthew 24:12

This is sad, but true. It sounds like today. Lord, help us. We need Your healing touch.

Ye have wearied the LORD with your words. Yet ye say, Wherein have we wearied him? When ye say, Every one that doeth evil is good in the sight of the LORD, and he delighteth in them; or, Where is the God of judgment? Malachi 2:17

I wonder if God is tired of our immorality and ammorality. Let's get back to the never changing right and wrong morality of the Bible. It's the only way a nation can survive.

Wherefore we receiving a kingdom which cannot be moved, let us have grace, whereby we may serve God acceptably with reverence and godly fear: For our God is a consuming fire. Hebrews 12:28-29

Christians need a revival of respect for God. He is our best friend, but don't forget that He is the same One who made this universe. Love the Lord with respect.

And when they brought out the money that was brought into the house of the LORD, Hilkiah the priest found a book of the law of the LORD given by Moses. 2 Chronicles 34:14

The finding and reading of this book of the law brought revival in that day. I believe it will do the same today. Read the Bible and believe it. Revival can be yours.

Ye shall not respect persons in judgment; but ye shall hear the small as well as the great; ye shall not be afraid of the face of man; for the judgment is God's. Deuteronomy 1:17

Real justice can never be accomplished until we accept and practice God's moral law. Our world needs a revival of Godly justice.

And it came to pass, when the king had heard the words of the book of the law, that he rent his clothes. 2 Kings 22:11

King Josiah tore his clothes in anguish when he heard the Word of God. He realized how sinful he and his nation had become. This sounds like the kind of revival we need all across our land. Read the Word of God and let God speak to you.

And Isaac digged again the wells of water, which they had digged in the days of Abraham his father; for the Philistines had stopped them after the death of Abraham: and he called their names after the names by which his father had called them.
Genesis 26:18

Is it time for us to redig some spiritual wells that were dug by our fathers? Let's get back to the old-time religion of reading the Bible and prayer. Our society desperately needs it.

If my people, which are called by my name, shall humble themselves, and pray, and seek my face, and turn from their wicked ways; then will I hear from heaven, and will forgive their sin, and will heal their land. 2 Chronicles 7:14

Revival always begins with repentance of sin. Are you in need of revival? Follow the instructions of this verse.

Then Jacob said unto his household, and to all that were with him, Put away the strange gods that are among you, and be clean, and change your garments: And let us arise, and go up to Bethel; and I will make there an altar unto God, who answered me in the day of my distress, and was with me in the way which I went. Genesis 35:2-3

Something similar to these verses needs to take place among many of God's people today. Lord, send a revival.

And even as they did not like to retain God in their knowledge, God gave them over to a reprobate mind, to do those things which are not convenient; Romans 1:28

I'm concerned. Our society reflects this verse. Lord, send a revival.

Pure religion and undefiled before God and the Father is this, To visit the fatherless and widows in their affliction, and to keep himself unspotted from the world. James 1:27

We need a revival of pure religion in our world. Let's honor the Lord in word and deed.

O LORD, though our iniquities testify against us, do thou it for thy name's sake: for our backslidings are many; we have sinned against thee. Jeremiah 14:7

We need this same kind of revival praying today. May God have mercy on our land.

O LORD, I have heard thy speech, and was afraid: O LORD, revive thy work in the midst of the years, in the midst of the years make known; in wrath remember mercy. Habakkuk 3:2

Lord, this is my prayer for the sin-sick world. Lord send a revival. Will you join me in prayer for the urgent need of revival?

And this is the condemnation, that light is come into the world, and men loved darkness rather than light, because their deeds were evil. John 3:19

We live in such a day today. People would rather embrace the darkness of hatred and immorality than that of love and holiness. Lord, send a revival.

And Samuel spake unto all the house of Israel, saying, If ye do return unto the LORD with all your hearts, then put away the strange gods and Ashtaroth from among you, and prepare your hearts unto the LORD, and serve him only: and he will deliver you out of the hand of the Philistines. Then the children of Israel did put away Baalim and Ashtaroth, and served the LORD only.
1 Samuel 7:3-4

Are we willing to put away the things that keep us from serving the Lord? That's the key to true revival.

In whom the god of this world hath blinded the minds of them which believe not, lest the light of the glorious gospel of Christ, who is the image of God, should shine unto them. 2 Corinthians 4:4

There is indeed no other explanation to the moral foolishness and depravity of our day. Lord, send a revival.

Woe unto them that call evil good, and good evil;
that put darkness for light, and light for darkness;
that put bitter for sweet, and sweet for bitter!
Isaiah 5:20

It is obvious that we live in such a day as this. We need a revival of faith in God soon or it will be too late for us.

Having therefore these promises, dearly beloved, let
us cleanse ourselves from all filthiness of the flesh
and spirit, perfecting holiness in the fear of God.
2 Corinthians 7:1

This is the kind of revival we need today. Let's reject sin and clothe ourselves in God's holiness.

This know also, that in the last days perilous times
shall come. For men shall be lovers of their own
selves, covetous, boasters, proud, blasphemers,
disobedient to parents, unthankful, unholy,
2 Timothy 3:1-2

If these aren't the last days, they sure look like them. Lord, send a revival. We need you.

Wilt thou not revive us again: that thy people may rejoice in thee? Psalm 85:6

May our hearts become this hungry for God. We need a revival now.

For they have healed the hurt of the daughter of my people slightly, saying, Peace, peace; when there is no peace. Jeremiah 8:11

We don't need pious platitudes from our spiritual leaders. We need the Word of God straight and pure. We need a revival.

Having a form of godliness, but denying the power thereof: from such turn away. 2 Timothy 3:5

We have fancy church buildings, good music, programs, etc. Yet, where is the power? Let's fall on our knees and ask the Lord to send revival fire.

Salvation

And Zacchaeus stood, and said unto the Lord; Behold, Lord, the half of my goods I give to the poor; and if I have taken any thing from any man by false accusation, I restore him fourfold. Luke 19:8

When Jesus is given entrance to your heart and home He makes a wonderful difference. Is He in your heart and home?

And he said unto him, If they hear not Moses and the prophets, neither will they be persuaded, though one rose from the dead. Luke 16:31

If you're waiting for that bolt of lightning or for an angel to whisper in your ear before you become a Christian, you've made a terrible mistake. If you won't put your trust in Jesus and the Word of God alone you'll never be saved. Trust Him today.

Many will say to me in that day, Lord, Lord, have we not prophesied in thy name? and in thy name have cast out devils? and in thy name done many wonderful works? And then will I profess unto them, I never knew you: depart from me, ye that work iniquity. Matthew 7:22-23

Going through the rudiments of religion does not guarantee a relationship to Jesus. Personal faith and trust in Him is the only way of salvation. Have you given Him your life?

Likewise, I say unto you, there is joy in the presence of the angels of God over one sinner that repenteth. Luke 15:10

Could it be that today you would set the angels to rejoicing? Give your life to Jesus. He loves you.

Call unto me, and I will answer thee, and shew thee great and mighty things, which thou knowest not. Jeremiah 33:3

God is wanting to do something wonderful in your life. Call on Him and see Him make things happen.

No servant can serve two masters: for either he will hate the one, and love the other; or else he will hold to the one, and despise the other. Ye cannot serve God and mammon. Luke 16:13

It can't be any clearer than this! Who or what is your God?

For by grace are ye saved through faith; and that not of yourselves: it is the gift of God: Not of works, lest any man should boast. Ephesians 2:8-9

We cannot work or earn our way to Heaven. We are saved by God's wonderful grace.

And I will restore to you the years that the locust hath eaten, the cankerworm, and the caterpiller, and the palmerworm, my great army which I sent among you. Joel 2:25

God can make up for the wasted years in your life. Put your life in His hands and watch Him work.

Enter ye in at the strait gate: for wide is the gate, and broad is the way, that leadeth to destruction, and many there be which go in thereat: Because strait is the gate, and narrow is the way, which leadeth unto life, and few there be that find it.
Matthew 7:13-14

What is this narrow gate to life? It is through Jesus-the way, the truth, and the life; "no man cometh unto the Father, but by me." (John 14:6)

And they said, Believe on the Lord Jesus Christ, and thou shalt be saved, and thy house. Acts 16:31

Put your trust in Jesus. He will save you from your sins and from Hell. He loves you.

In my Father's house are many mansions: if it were not so, I would have told you. I go to prepare a place for you. And if I go and prepare a place for you, I will come again, and receive you unto myself; that where I am, there ye may be also. John 14:2-3

Heaven awaits God's people. Have you given your life to Jesus? He's the only way to Heaven.

Come now, and let us reason together, saith the
LORD: though your sins be as scarlet, they shall be
as white as snow; though they be red like crimson,
they shall be as wool. Isaiah 1:18

You don't have to continue to carry that load of guilt.
Confess your sins to the Lord and let Him make you
new.

What shall we say then? Shall we continue in sin,
that grace may abound? God forbid. How shall we,
that are dead to sin, live any longer therein?
Romans 6:1-2

Salvation by grace is not a license to sin. It's a call to
live a holy life.

While we look not at the things which are seen, but
at the things which are not seen: for the things which
are seen are temporal; but the things which are not
seen are eternal. 2 Corinthians 4:18

This gives us a handle on reality. Our bodies will one
day cease but our souls will go into eternity. Are you
ready to face God?

Therefore if any man be in Christ, he is a new creature: old things are passed away; behold, all things are become new. 2 Corinthains 5:17

Jesus specializes in giving people new beginnings. Give your life to Him and watch Him work.

So the posts passed from city to city through the country of Ephraim and Manasseh even unto Zebulun: but they laughed them to scorn, and mocked them. Nevertheless divers of Asher and Manasseh and of Zebulun humbled themselves, and came to Jerusalem. 2 Chronicles 30:10-11

Do you reject the invitation of God or do you accept it? Come to the Lord. He loves you.

In those days was Hezekiah sick unto death. And Isaiah the prophet the son of Amoz came unto him, and said unto him, Thus saith the LORD, Set thine house in order: for thou shalt die, and not live. Isaiah 38:1

Is your house in order? Are you ready to meet the Lord? You can be. Give your whole life to Him.

And when these things begin to come to pass, then look up, and lift up your heads; for your redemption draweth nigh. Luke 21:28

Are you paying attention to what's going on around you? Think about it. His coming may be soon. Are you ready? "Lift up your heads; for your redemption draweth nigh."

Remember ye not the former things, neither consider the things of old. Behold, I will do a new thing; now it shall spring forth; shall ye not know it? I will even make a way in the wilderness, and rivers in the desert. Isaiah 43:18-19

The Lord can give you a new start also. Don't let the past drag you down. Move forward with the Lord.

Behold, I stand at the door, and knock: if any man hear my voice, and open the door, I will come in to him, and will sup with him, and he with me. Revelation 3:20

Jesus is anxious to gain entry to your life. He is what all people need. Open your life to Him.

*As for me, I will call upon God; and the LORD shall
save me. Psalm 55:16*

The Lord will come to your rescue too, if you surrender your all to Him.

*Thou art worthy, O Lord, to receive glory and
honour and power: for thou hast created all things,
and for thy pleasure they are and were created.
Revelation 4:11*

This picture of the future certainly puts life into perspective. Get in touch with reality. Put your life into the hands of Jesus.

*We then, as workers together with him, beseech you
also that ye receive not the grace of God in vain.
(For he saith, I have heard thee in a time accepted,
and in the day of salvation have I succoured thee:
behold, now is the accepted time; behold, now is the
day of salvation.) 2 Corinthians 6:1-2*

Don't put it off another minute. Give your life completely to Jesus.

For the wages of sin is death; but the gift of God is
eternal life through Jesus Christ our Lord.
Romans 6:23

You have an important choice to make. Will you
chance facing God with your sin and its consequences
or will you accept God's gift of salvation? You must
choose.

And if Christ be not raised, your faith is vain; ye are
yet in your sins. 1 Corinthians 15:17

The central message of the Gospel is that Jesus did
rise from the dead. We serve a risen Savior. Do you
know Him?

For out of the heart proceed evil thoughts, murders,
adulteries, fornications, thefts, false witness,
blasphemies. Matthew 15:19

Man is not good by nature. We are all sinners. Let
Jesus give you a new heart and new attitude. We all
need Him.

*As he came forth of his mother's womb, naked shall
he return to go as he came, and shall take nothing of
his labour, which he may carry away in his hand.*
Ecclesiastes 5:15

This certainly makes us think. The things that last are
those things which are eternal. Are you ready to face
eternity?

*For what is a man profited, if he shall gain the whole
world, and lose his own soul? or what shall a man
give in exchange for his soul? Matthew 16:26*

Have you sold your soul for the temporary, fleeting
things and pleasures of this world? Wake up.
Surrender your life to Jesus before it's too late.

*The heart is deceitful above all things, and
desperately wicked: who can know it?*
Jeremiah 17:9

Man is not innately good. The Bible says that man is
a sinner. Give that old heart to God and let Him make
you new.

*For whosoever shall call upon the name of the Lord
shall be saved. Romans 10:13*

This is the greatest offer made to mankind. Have you
accepted it?

*Neither is there salvation in any other: for there is
none other name under heaven given among men,
whereby we must be saved. Acts 4:12*

Salvation only comes in the name of Jesus. Have you
called upon Him to be your Savior? He loves you!

*So then every one of us shall give account of himself
to God. Romans 14:12*

No one is exempt from God's audit. Are you ready to
face God? You can be if you know Jesus.

*When Jesus therefore had received the vinegar, he
said, It is finished: and he bowed his head,
and gave up the ghost. John 19:30*

This is not a cry of defeat but a shout of victory. God's plan of salvation was accomplished when Jesus died on the cross. Praise the Lord! It is finished!

These things have I written unto you that believe on the name of the Son of God; that ye may know that ye have eternal life, and that ye may believe on the name of the Son of God. 1 John 5:13

Our salvation is not built on guesswork or "hope-so." We can know we are secure in Christ because we placed our faith Him. If you've done this rejoice. You're a child of the King.

Many will say to me in that day, Lord, Lord, have we not prophesied in thy name? and in thy name have cast out devils? and in thy name done many wonderful works? And then will I profess unto them, I never knew you: depart from me, ye that work iniquity. Matthew 7:22-23

Going through the rudiments of religion does not guarantee a relationship to Jesus. Personal faith and trust in Him is the only way of salvation. Have you given Him your life?

*For all have sinned, and come short of the glory
of God. Romans 3:23*

You and I are just not good enough to get to heaven.
We are sinners. This is why we need Jesus. He died
for us so that we might live with Him.

*But as it is written, Eye hath not seen, nor ear heard,
neither have entered into the heart of man, the things
which God hath prepared for them that love him.
1 Corinthians 2:9*

Do you love the Lord? If not, you are robbing yourself of the greatest blessing of life. Jesus said that He
came to give you life abundant. Give your life to Him.

*For the mystery of iniquity doth already work: only
he who now letteth will let, until he be taken out of
the way. And then shall that Wicked be revealed,
whom the Lord shall consume with the spirit of his
mouth, and shall destroy with the brightness of his
coming: 2 Thessalonians 2:7-8*

Picture a world that has not one ounce of the presence
of the Holy Spirit. It's going to happen when Jesus

comes back for His people. Are you ready, or will you be left behind?

For the invisible things of him from the creation of the world are clearly seen, being understood by the things that are made, even his eternal power and Godhead; so that they are without excuse:
Romans 1:20

There is no excuse for not knowing the Lord. He will take control of your life if you will ask. Why don't you pray right now to accept Him as your Lord and Savior.

For bodily exercise profiteth little: but godliness is profitable unto all things, having promise of the life that now is, and of that which is to come.
1 Timothy 4:8

Are you in shape? I mean, are you in spiritual shape? This old body will one day give way but the soul goes on into eternity. Are you ready to face the Lord? You can be. Give your life to Jesus.

Behold, all souls are mine; as the soul of the father, so also the soul of the son is mine: the soul that sinneth, it shall die. Ezekiel 18:4

Sin has terrible, eternal consequences and yet there is hope. "For the wages of sin is death; but the gift of God is eternal life through Jesus Christ our Lord." (Romans 6:23) Give your life to the Lord.

Can any hide himself in secret places that I shall not see him? saith the LORD. Do not I fill heaven and earth? saith the LORD. Jeremiah 23:24

You can try as hard as you want but you cannot hide from God. The Lord has your best interests at heart. Why not come to Him and see what He can do in you.

But whosoever drinketh of the water that I shall give him shall never thirst; but the water that I shall give him shall be in him a well of water springing up into everlasting life. John 4:14

Is your soul empty and dry? Jesus can bring life and vitality to your life. Let Him give you a life that satisfies.

*And he said unto him, If they hear not Moses and
the prophets, neither will they be persuaded, though
one rose from the dead. Luke 16:31*

If you're waiting for that bolt of lightning or for an
angel to whisper in your ear before you become a
Christian, you've made a terrible mistake. If you
won't put your trust in Jesus and the Word of God
alone you'll never be saved. Trust Him today.

*And she brought forth her firstborn son, and
wrapped him in swaddling clothes, and laid him
in a manger; because there was no room for
them in the inn. Luke 2:7*

Do you have any room for Jesus? He has room for
you. He has much more to give you than what you
could give Him. Make room for Jesus.

*And these shall go away into everlasting
punishment: but the righteous into life eternal.
Matthew 25:46*

Where are you headed? Are you going to everlasting
punishment or life eternal? It all depends on what you

do with Jesus. Will you trust Him and experience life eternal?

I say unto you, that likewise joy shall be in heaven over one sinner that repenteth, more than over ninety and nine just persons, which need no repentance.
Luke 15:7

Have you brought joy to Heaven yet? You can by giving your life to Jesus. By the way, you'll bring great joy to your own heart.

Therefore we conclude that a man is justified by faith without the deeds of the law. Romans 3:28

No one is good enough to enter Heaven by his good works. This is why we need Jesus. He died for us so that we could be saved from Hell. Have you asked Him to save you?

For in him dwelleth all the fulness of the Godhead bodily. And ye are complete in him, which is the

head of all principality and power.
Colossians 2:9-10

Jesus has a way of making our lives complete. Is something missing in your life? Have you given your life to Jesus? He's the key to real living.

Neither do men put new wine into old bottles: else the bottles break, and the wine runneth out, and the bottles perish: but they put new wine into new bottles, and both are preserved. Matthew 9:17

The salvation experience is not a patching up of the old. It is a brand new life given to those who trust Jesus.

How shall we escape, if we neglect so great salvation; which at the first began to be spoken by the Lord, and was confirmed unto us by them that heard him. Hebrews 2:3

Don't think that you can ignore God and suffer no consequences. He loves you. He died for your sins. Let Him be your Savior and Lord today.

And almost all things are by the law purged with blood; and without shedding of blood is no remission. Hebrews 9:22

"What can wash away my sin? Nothing but the blood of Jesus. What can make me whole again? Nothing but the blood of Jesus." The great old hymn says it all.

For whosoever shall call upon the name of the Lord shall be saved. Romans 10:13

You too can become a child of God. Claim this promise for your life.

Boast not thyself of to morrow; for thou knowest not what a day may bring forth. Proverbs 27:1

Trust the Lord with your life today. You may not have tomorrow.

Who his own self bare our sins in his own body on the tree, that we, being dead to sins, should live unto

righteousness: by whose stripes ye were healed.
1 Peter 2:24

Don't forget. Christ died for you. He arose from the dead to live in you. Let Jesus be the Lord of your life.

Come unto me, all ye that labour and are heavy laden, and I will give you rest. Take my yoke upon you, and learn of me; for I am meek and lowly in heart: and ye shall find rest unto your souls.For my yoke is easy, and my burden is light.
Matthew 11:28-30

This is a personal invitation from Jesus to you. Will you accept?

And they that passed by reviled him, wagging their heads, And saying, Thou that destroyest the temple, and buildest it in three days, save thyself. If thou be the Son of God, come down from the cross.
Matthew 27:39-40

It's precisely because Jesus is the Son of God that He did not come down from the cross. He came to die for our sins.

Then spake Jesus again unto them, saying, I am the light of the world: he that followeth me shall not walk in darkness, but shall have the light of life.
John 8:12

Are you tired of walking in spiritual darkness? Come to the light. Come to Jesus.

Therefore be ye also ready: for in such an hour as ye think not the Son of man cometh. Matthew 24:44

Jesus could come back to earth any day. Are you ready? "Which also, Ye men of Galilee, why stand ye gazing up into heaven? This same Jesus, which is taken up from you into heaven, shall so come in like manner as ye have seen him go into heaven." (Acts 1:11)

And the lord said unto the servant, Go out into the highways and hedges, and compel them to come in, that my house may be filled. Luke 14:23

God wants you to be a part of His family. There's always room for one more.

*And whatsoever ye shall ask in my name, that will
I do, that the Father may be glorified in the Son.
If ye shall ask any thing in my name, I will do it.
John 14:13-14*

Is your life empty? Jesus gives life that abundantly
satisfies.

*If the Son therefore shall make you free, ye shall be
free indeed. John 8:36*

Jesus can set you free from the sin that has you in
bondage. Surrender your life to Him now.

*All that the Father giveth me shall come to me; and
him that cometh to me I will in no wise cast out.
John 6:37*

Come to Jesus. Trust Him. He will not turn you away.

*He that rejecteth me, and receiveth not my words,
hath one that judgeth him: the word that I have*

spoken, the same shall judge him in the last day.
John 12:48

Judgment is reality. Those who reject Jesus will have to answer to the Heavenly Father. Trust Jesus with your life before it's too late.

And Jesus said unto them, I am the bread of life: he that cometh to me shall never hunger; and he that believeth on me shall never thirst. John 6:35

Jesus can satisfy the longing of your soul. Give Him your life.

Behold, I stand at the door, and knock: if any man hear my voice, and open the door, I will come in to him, and will sup with him, and he with me.
Revelation 3:20

Is Jesus at your heart's door? Open your heart to Him. It's the opportunity of a lifetime.

The LORD killeth, and maketh alive: he bringeth down to the grave, and bringeth up. The LORD maketh poor, and maketh rich: he bringeth low, and lifteth up. 1 Samuel 2:6-7

The Lord keeps the final books on people. Where do you stand?

But though he had done so many miracles before them, yet they believed not on him. John 12:37

Think about it. Has Jesus done wonderful things for you and yet your are reluctant to follow Him? Give Him your whole life.

Jesus answered and said unto him, Verily, verily, I say unto thee, Except a man be born again, he cannot see the kingdom of God. John 3:3

Being born again is no option. It is a necessity to go to Heaven. Have you been born again?

He that believeth on me, as the scripture hath said,
out of his belly shall flow rivers of living water.
John 7:38

Has your life run dry? Let Jesus bring streams of living water into your life.

Sharing the
Good News

Let the righteous smite me; it shall be a kindness:
and let him reprove me; it shall be an excellent oil,
which shall not break my head. Psalm 141:5

A godly friend who will share the truth with you is a
friend indeed. It may sometimes sting, but it will be a
blessing to your life.

And daily in the temple, and in every house, they
ceased not to teach and preach Jesus Christ.
Acts 5:42

Everyday should be a day that we tell others about
Jesus. Share the Good News of Christ with someone
today.

For whosoever shall be ashamed of me and of my words, of him shall the Son of man be ashamed, when he shall come in his own glory, and in his Father's, and of the holy angels. Luke 9:26

If we are ashamed of Jesus on earth how will we ever be comfortable in Heaven to spend an eternity with Him? Don't be ashamed. Tell others that you belong to Him.

And I saw another angel fly in the midst of heaven, having the everlasting gospel to preach unto them that dwell on the earth, and to every nation, and kindred, and tongue, and people." Revelation 14:6

We cannot rest until the gospel is shared with the whole world. What are you doing to attain this worthy goal?

Then I said, I will not make mention of him, nor speak any more in his name. But his word was in mine heart as a burning fire shut up in my bones, and I was weary with forbearing, and I could not stay. Jeremiah 20:9

We all need to be filled with the Lord's message and the Lord's will. May our lives be a shining witness for Him. Let His Word be a fire in your soul.

Woe unto you, when all men shall speak well of you! for so did their fathers to the false prophets.
Luke 6:26

Making a stand for the Lord will not always make you the most popular person. Remember, they crucified Jesus. Be bold for the Lord.

Then saith he unto his disciples, The harvest truly is plenteous, but the labourers are few; Pray ye therefore the Lord of the harvest, that he will send forth labourers into his harvest. Matthew 9:37-38

Are you a side-line Christian? Get in the game. Tell others about Jesus.

Whosoever therefore shall confess me before men, him will I confess also before my Father which is in

heaven. But whosoever shall deny me before men,
him will I also deny before my Father which is in
heaven. Matthew 10:32-33

It is essential to publicly profess Jesus before others.
Don't be ashamed of belonging to Jesus. It is a privilege.

But ye shall receive power, after that the Holy Ghost
is come upon you: and ye shall be witnesses unto me
both in Jerusalem, and in all Judaea, and in
Samaria, and unto the uttermost part of the earth.
Acts 1:8

The Lord will empower His people to tell the Good
News of Jesus. Tell someone today about Him.

If any man speak, let him speak as the oracles of
God; if any man minister, let him do it as of the
ability which God giveth: that God in all things may
be glorified through Jesus Christ, to whom be praise
and dominion for ever and ever. Amen. 1 Peter 4:11

The purpose of our lives is to point all to Jesus. Praise
the Lord!

Then Peter said, Silver and gold have I none; but
such as I have give I thee: In the name of Jesus
Christ of Nazareth rise up and walk. Acts 3:6

Jesus can give us just what we need. Let us share Him
with others.

The same came therefore to Philip, which was of
Bethsaida of Galilee, and desired him, saying, Sir,
we would see Jesus. John 12:21

People have seen enough religious traditions. They
long to see Jesus. Live for Jesus and point others to
Him.

That if thou shalt confess with thy mouth the Lord
Jesus, and shalt believe in thine heart that God hath
raised him from the dead, thou shalt be saved. For
with the heart man believeth unto righteousness; and
with the mouth confession is made unto salvation.
Romans 10:9-10

People who believe in Jesus are not ashamed to confess Him before others. Tell others about your faith in
the Lord.

Let not then your good be evil spoken of.
Romans 14:16

God's people must "speak up." Stand up for Jesus and His Word.

For we preach not ourselves, but Christ Jesus the Lord; and ourselves your servants for Jesus' sake.
2 Corinthians 4:5

People do not need to hear pious platitudes. The world needs to hear about Jesus.

And with great power gave the apostles witness of the resurrection of the Lord Jesus: and great grace was upon them all. Acts 4:33

The message of the cross and resurrection is a powerful one. Let's share it!

But sanctify the Lord God in your hearts: and be ready always to give an answer to every man that

asketh you a reason of the hope that is in you with
meekness and fear: 1 Peter 3:15

People need hope. People need the Lord. Christian, share your faith. People are counting on you.

Let the redeemed of the LORD say so, whom he hath redeemed from the hand of the enemy; Psalm 107:2

Speak up for God. He's done much for you. People need to hear what you have to share.

Return to thine own house, and shew how great things God hath done unto thee. And he went his way, and published throughout the whole city how great things Jesus had done unto him. Luke 8:39

Have you told anyone lately what Jesus means to you? Many need Him. Share the Good News.

And when they could not come nigh unto him for the press, they uncovered the roof where he was: and

when they had broken it up, they let down the bed
wherein the sick of the palsy lay.   Mark 2:4

These men would not let any obstacle keep them from bringing their sick friend to Jesus. Christians need the same sense of urgency and concern today. Bring a friend to Jesus.

Restore unto me the joy of thy salvation; and uphold
me with thy free spirit. Then will I teach
transgressors thy ways; and sinners shall be
converted unto thee. Psalm 51:12-13

If you have been saved by the grace of God, have you taken time to tell others about His salvation? Ask the Lord to give you a burden for souls.

And when thy son asketh thee in time to come,
saying, What mean the testimonies, and the statutes,
and the judgments, which the LORD our God hath
commanded you? Deuteronomy 6:20

Parents, take time to tell your children about the Lord. They need to know what the Lord means to you.

*Howbeit Jesus suffered him not, but saith unto him,
Go home to thy friends, and tell them how great
things the Lord hath done for thee, and hath had
compassion on thee. Mark 5:19*

Jesus needs more people telling others about Him.
Invite a friend to Bible study and church. Show them
the way of Jesus.

*Then said Jesus to them again, Peace be unto you:
as my Father hath sent me, even so send I you.
John 20:21*

Christians, let's remember what God wants us to do.
Don't become self-centered but rather become other-
centered. Tell someone about Jesus today.

*Then took Mary a pound of ointment of spikenard,
very costly, and anointed the feet of Jesus, and wiped
his feet with her hair: and the house was filled with
the odour of the ointment. John 12:3*

People in love with Jesus need to show the world that
they do. Christian, what have you done to show your
love for Him?

But if our gospel be hid, it is hid to them that are lost: 2 Corinthians 4:3

Christianity was never meant to be a secret or closed society. We have good news to tell a world that is desperately searching. Share Jesus with a friend.

That this may be a sign among you, that when your children ask their fathers in time to come, saying, What mean ye by these stones? Then ye shall answer them, That the waters of Jordan were cut off before the ark of the covenant of the LORD; when it passed over Jordan, the waters of Jordan were cut off: and these stones shall be for a memorial unto the children of Israel for ever. Joshua 4:6-7

Are our children seeing an evidence of the work of the Lord in our lives? Share with your children what the Lord means to you.

For I am not ashamed of the gospel of Christ: for it is the power of God unto salvation to every one that believeth; to the Jew first, and also to the Greek. Romans 1:16

The gospel is this. We are all sinners and lost from God. Jesus died for our sins and arose from the dead to bring forgiveness of sin for those who believe. It's no wonder that gospel means good news.

And when they found them not, they drew Jason and certain brethren unto the rulers of the city, crying, These that have turned the world upside down are come hither also; Acts 17:6

If Christians would start turning this world upside down it would finally become right side up. Christians, stand on the Bible. Share Jesus with others.

For our gospel came not unto you in word only, but also in power, and in the Holy Ghost, and in much assurance; as ye know what manner of men we were among you for your sake. 1 Thessalonians 1:5

How is our gospel coming over to other people? Are we doing more than just saying words? Let's live a life pleasing to God.

As cold waters to a thirsty soul, so is good news
from a far country. Proverbs 25:25

Many people have yet to hear of God's love for their
lives. What are you doing to let others know? Lead
them to the One who satisfies.

Therefore they that were scattered abroad went every
where preaching the word. Acts 8:4

All of us can be a witness for Jesus wherever we go.
When was the last time you talked to someone about
trusting the Lord? Tell someone today.

And Philip ran thither to him, and heard him read
the prophet Esaias, and said, Understandest thou
what thou readest? And he said, How can I, except
some man should guide me? And he desired Philip
that he would come up and sit with him.
Acts 8:30-31

Christian, how many others are waiting to hear and
understand the Good News of Jesus? We must be willing and available to share Him with others.

Then shall he answer them, saying, Verily I say unto you, Inasmuch as ye did it not to one of the least of these, ye did it not to me. Matthew 25:45

The Christian life is a sharing life. If each one of us share with those in need we can make a difference. If we don't, we violate Christ's teaching for our lives.

Declare his glory among the heathen; his marvellous works among all nations. 1 Chronicles 16:24

It is the joy and the responsibility of all God's people to share Him with others. Tell someone about the Lord today.

Go ye therefore, and teach all nations, baptizing them in the name of the Father, and of the Son, and of the Holy Ghost: Matthew 28:19

Have we forgotten that there's a world that needs Jesus? Jesus hasn't. Let's quit majoring on the minors and win people to Jesus.

For we cannot but speak the things which we have seen and heard. Acts 4:20

Dear Christian, don't hold it in any longer. Tell the Good News of Jesus. People need the Lord!

Restore unto me the joy of thy salvation; and uphold me with thy free spirit. Then will I teach transgressors thy ways; and sinners shall be converted unto thee. Psalm 51:12-13

After we experience God's forgiveness we should want to share Him with others.

And he said unto them, What man shall there be among you, that shall have one sheep, and if it fall into a pit on the sabbath day, will he not lay hold on it, and lift it out? How much then is a man better than a sheep? Wherefore it is lawful to do well on the sabbath days. Matthew 12:11-12

In the quest to save the environment we must never forget that the lives of people must be our first concern. Take time to share the Lord with someone today.

Ye are our epistle written in our hearts, known and read of all men: 2 Corinthians 3:2

Christian, you may be the only gospel someone ever reads. Live your life for Jesus so that others may come to know Him too.

And as it is appointed unto men once to die, but after this the judgment: So Christ was once offered to bear the sins of many; and unto them that look for him shall he appear the second time without sin unto salvation. Hebrews 9:27-28

Do we believe what these verses say? If so, we should do all in our power to share Christ with a lost and dying world.

And now, Lord, behold their threatenings: and grant unto thy servants, that with all boldness they may speak thy word, Acts 4:29

We must boldly pray if we are to be bold witnesses for Jesus. God will answer our prayer if we really mean business.

Also I say unto you, Whosoever shall confess me before men, him shall the Son of man also confess before the angels of God: But he that denieth me before men shall be denied before the angels of God. Luke 12:8-9

A person who knows Jesus is glad to tell others. Do you know Him?

Now then we are ambassadors for Christ, as though God did beseech you by us: we pray you in Christ's stead, be ye reconciled to God. 2 Corinthians 5:20

Man is in need of being reconciled to God. Christian, we are the Lord's ambassadors to hurting people. Take time to share Jesus with someone today.

According to my earnest expectation and my hope, that in nothing I shall be ashamed, but that with all boldness, as always, so now also Christ shall be magnified in my body, whether it be by life, or by death. Philippians 1:20

This should be the heartbeat of every Christian. Let's be bold for God. Let others see Jesus in you.

We will not hide them from their children, shewing to the generation to come the praises of the LORD, and his strength, and his wonderful works that he hath done. Psalm 78:4

Parents, are you taking time to tell your children about the Lord? Pass the Good News of God's Word on to your children.

For God so loved the world, that he gave his only begotten Son, that whosoever believeth in him should not perish, but have everlasting life. John 3:16

This is the greatest love story ever told. Believe it and share it with others.

And also all that generation were gathered unto their fathers: and there arose another generation after them, which knew not the LORD, nor yet the works which he had done for Israel. Judges 2:10

It so important to pass our faith in the Lord on to our children. Take time to share the Lord with your family.

He first findeth his own brother Simon, and saith unto him, We have found the Messias, which is, being interpreted, the Christ. John 1:41

Take time to share Jesus with someone you love. That's the greatest gift you could ever share with them.

Let the redeemed of the LORD say so, whom he hath redeemed from the hand of the enemy; Psalm 107:2

People are longing to hear from those who have experienced God's grace. Pass the faith to someone today.

Now the man out of whom the devils were departed besought him that he might be with him: but Jesus sent him away, saying, Return to thine own house, and shew how great things God hath done unto thee. And he went his way, and published throughout the whole city how great things Jesus had done unto him. Luke 8:38-39

It is important to tell those closest to us how much Jesus means to us. Have you shared Jesus with your family and friends?

The fruit of the righteous is a tree of life; and he that winneth souls is wise. Proverbs 11:30

Pointing others to the Lord is an act of wisdom and also an act of kindness. Tell someone about Him today.

Thanksgiving and Praise

For ye know the grace of our Lord Jesus Christ, that, though he was rich, yet for your sakes he became poor, that ye through his poverty might be rich.
2 Corinthians 8:9

Jesus gave His all for us. Thank you Jesus.

And there came a voice from heaven, saying, Thou art my beloved Son, in whom I am well pleased.
Mark 1:11

I will say "Amen" to that. Jesus is a wonderful Savior! The Heavenly Father was exactly right. This same Jesus went to the cross for my sins and yours. Thank you, Jesus.

For he hath made him to be sin for us, who knew no sin; that we might be made the righteousness of God in him. 2 Corinthians 5:21

What an exchange! Jesus took our sin and gave us His righteousness. Thank you Jesus.

But God forbid that I should glory, save in the cross of our Lord Jesus Christ, by whom the world is crucified unto me, and I unto the world. Galatians 6:14

"My hope is built on nothing less than Jesus' blood and righteousness." I thank the Lord for dying for my sins on the cross.

For I know that my redeemer liveth, and that he shall stand at the latter day upon the earth: And though after my skin worms destroy this body, yet in my flesh shall I see God. Job 19:25-26

I praise God that my redeemer liveth. Do you know Him? He loves you.

But I will sing of thy power; yea, I will sing aloud of thy mercy in the morning: for thou hast been my defence and refuge in the day of my trouble.
Psalm 59:16

What a great way to begin the day. Take time to "Praise the Lord" the first thing every day.

And almost all things are by the law purged with blood; and without shedding of blood is no remission. Hebrews 9:22

We must never forget that our salvation was paid in full by Jesus on the cross. Praise the Lord!

In whom we have redemption through his blood, the forgiveness of sins, according to the riches of his grace. Ephesians 1:7

Let's don't forget that our salvation cost Jesus His life's blood. Take time to thank Him and praise Him.

From the rising of the sun unto the going down of the same the LORD's name is to be praised.
Psalm 113:3

When was the last time you had a good praise session that brought honor and glory to the Lord? Take time to praise Him now.

The heavens are thine, the earth also is thine: as for the world and the fulness thereof, thou hast founded them. Psalm 89:11

Life gets in proper focus when we realize that this world belongs to God. Give God the praise and glory for who He is.

Not unto us, O LORD, not unto us, but unto thy name give glory, for thy mercy, and for thy truth's sake.
Psalm 115:1

God is the one that deserves our praise. We are insignificant in comparison to Him. "To God be the glory, great things He has done."

Knowing that he which raised up the Lord Jesus shall raise up us also by Jesus, and shall present us with you. 2 Corinthians 4:14

Death is not the end of it all for the Christian. Our Lord conquered death for us. Rejoice, you're a child of the King of time and eternity.

The LORD hath done great things for us; whereof we are glad. Psalm 126:3

Let's be certain to give the Lord the glory and praise due Him. It's time. The Lord has done great things for us.

Pilate therefore said unto him, Art thou a king then? Jesus answered, Thou sayest that I am a king. To this end was I born, and for this cause came I into the world, that I should bear witness unto the truth. Every one that is of the truth heareth my voice. John 18:37

Don't forget that Jesus is King of Kings and Lord of Lords. Pilate has come and gone but Jesus still reigns. Worship the King!

But God commendeth his love toward us, in that,
while we were yet sinners, Christ died for us.
Romans 5:8

God loves us in spite of our failings. He loves us unconditionally. He proved it by sending Jesus to die for us. Thank you Lord for your wonderful love.

And the angel answered and said unto the women,
Fear not ye: for I know that ye seek Jesus, which was
crucified. He is not here: for he is risen, as he said.
Come, see the place where the Lord lay.
Matthew 28:5-6

Let's don't forget that we serve the resurrected Lord. He has conquered sin, death and the grave on our behalf. Thank you Jesus!

Be still, and know that I am God: I will be exalted
among the heathen, I will be exalted in the earth.
Psalm 46:10

Take time to reflect on what really counts. When you do you will rediscover that God is still on His throne. I'm thankful for that, aren't you?

But we have this treasure in earthen vessels, that the
excellency of the power may be of God, and not of us.
2 Corinthians 4:7

It's a privilege to have the Lord in our lives. He has
placed His love and power in our frail lives. Praise the
Lord!

But let him that glorieth glory in this, that he
understandeth and knoweth me, that I am the LORD
which exercise lovingkindness, judgment, and
righteousness, in the earth: for in these things I
delight, saith the LORD. Jeremiah 9:24

If we must brag, let's brag on the Lord. We can never
praise Him enough.

And one of them, when he saw that he was healed,
turned back, and with a loud voice glorified God,
And fell down on his face at his feet, giving him
thanks: and he was a Samaritan. Luke 17:15-16

Be sure to thank the Lord for all He has done for you.
Ingratitude is a sin.

*These wait all upon thee; that thou mayest give them
their meat in due season. Psalm 104:27*

Remember to thank the Lord for the food He provides. Take time to say grace before you eat your meal.

*But by the grace of God I am what I am: and his
grace which was bestowed upon me was not in vain;
but I laboured more abundantly than they all: yet not
I, but the grace of God which was with me.*
1 Corinthians 15:10

Thank the Lord for His amazing grace. His power can work wonders in all of our lives.

*He hath not dealt with us after our sins; nor
rewarded us according to our iniquities. For as the
heaven is high above the earth, so great is his mercy
toward them that fear him. As far as the east is from
the west, so far hath he removed our transgressions
from us. Psalm 103:10-12*

Thank you, Lord, for your wonderful forgiveness.

When I consider thy heavens, the work of thy fingers,
the moon and the stars, which thou hast ordained;
What is man, that thou art mindful of him? and the
son of man, that thou visitest him? Psalm 8:3-4

It's great to know that the Creator of the universe cares about us. Thank you Lord for loving us so much.

I exhort therefore, that, first of all, supplications,
prayers, intercessions, and giving of thanks, be made
for all men. 1 Timothy 2:1

What a great world this would be if we followed the teaching of this one verse. Let's try it. Let's pray for each other and thank God for each other.

But God forbid that I should glory, save in the cross
of our Lord Jesus Christ, by whom the world is
crucified unto me, and I unto the world.
Galatians 6:14

As Christians our glory is found in the old rugged cross where Jesus died for us. Take time now to thank the Lord for your salvation.

Wherefore I say unto thee, Her sins, which are many, are forgiven; for she loved much: but to whom little is forgiven, the same loveth little. Luke 7:47

Our love for the Lord increases when we realize just how merciful He has been to us. Thank you Lord for saving my soul.

And the people stood beholding. And the rulers also with them derided him, saying, He saved others; let him save himself, if he be Christ, the chosen of God. Luke 23:35

The reason He did not save Himself was so that He could save others. Hallelujah! Thank you Jesus for dying for a lost world.

O give thanks unto the LORD; for he is good: because his mercy endureth for ever. Psalm 118:1

When we take the Lord, other people and things for granted, we are the losers. Begin your day by thanking the Lord. You'll have a better day.

I am he that liveth, and was dead; and, behold, I am alive for evermore, Amen; and have the keys of hell and of death. Revelations 1:18

We serve a living Lord. We serve a powerful Lord. We serve a victorious Lord. Praise ye the Lord!

Bless the LORD, O my soul, and forget not all his benefits. Psalm 103:2

Don't forget all that the Lord has done for you. Take time to thank the Lord.

He shall not be afraid of evil tidings: his heart is fixed, trusting in the LORD. Psalm 112:7

God's people can face bad news because we have our trust ultimately in God. He can help us through any and every circumstance of life. Praise the Lord!

O give thanks unto the LORD; for he is good: for his mercy endureth for ever. Psalm 136:1

I join with the psalmist in thanking God for His goodness and mercy. Take time to thank God for all His blessings.

By him therefore let us offer the sacrifice of praise to God continually, that is, the fruit of our lips giving thanks to his name. Hebrews 13:15

Praise and thanksgiving to God should be a part of the life of Christians. Take time to express your appreciation to Him everyday.

But now is Christ risen from the dead, and become the firstfruits of them that slept. 1 Corinthians 15:20

Death does not enslave the Christian. Christ conquered death on our behalf. Praise the Lord! We serve a risen Savior. We too shall be resurrected to eternal life because He paved the way for us.

It is of the LORD's mercies that we are not consumed, because his compassions fail not. Lamentations 3:22

Here is the answer to why God puts up with so much. Thank you Lord for being so merciful and loving.

Bless the Lord, O my soul: and all that is within me, bless his holy name. Bless the Lord, O my soul, and forget not all his benefits. Psalm 103:1-2

Take time right now to remember all of God's blessings in your life. It's refreshing, isn't it? Praise the Lord for His goodness.

Not by works of righteousness which we have done, but according to his mercy he saved us, by the washing of regeneration, and renewing of the Holy Ghost. Titus 3:5

We can't take credit for our salvation. "Jesus paid it all." Thank you Lord for your wonderful mercy and love.

I laid me down and slept; I awaked; for the Lord sustained me. Psalm 3:5

We need to thank the Lord for every day. It is a gift from Him. Don't take life for granted. Give your best for the Lord.

Blessed be the Lord, who daily loadeth us with benefits, even the God of our salvation. Selah. Psalm 68:19

Isn't it good to know that God doesn't just check on us from time to time? He is there every day. Thank you Lord for your faithfulness.

They soon forgat his works; they waited not for his counsel: Psalm 106:13

Don't be guilty of forgetting the Lord and all His blessings. Continue to thank Him daily.

And Abraham called the name of that place Jehovah-jireh: as it is said to this day, In the mount of the Lord it shall be seen. Genesis 22:14

Jehovah-jireh means the Lord will provide. Look back on your life and recall how many times God has met your need and more. Now, give Him the praise and thanks He deserves.

Whom God hath raised up, having loosed the pains of death: because it was not possible that he should be holden of it. Acts 2:24

Death could not hold our Lord Jesus. Because of His victory those who know Him will not be chained to it either. Praise the Lord for the glorious resurrections.

I, even I, am he that blotteth out thy transgressions for mine own sake, and will not remember thy sins. Isaiah 43:25

I thank the Lord that He forgives our sins when we confess them and repent. It's wonderful to know Him.

I thank my God, making mention of thee always in my prayers. Philemon 1:4

Be thankful! Be thankful for others. It makes life much more enjoyable.

Continue in prayer, and watch in the same with thanksgiving. Colossians 4:2

This verse lists two things that are lacking in many lives today. They are prayer and thankfulness. Are they lacking in your life? If so, begin today to make them a priority in your life.

Notwithstanding in this rejoice not, that the spirits are subject unto you; but rather rejoice, because your names are written in heaven. Luke 10:20

If you're a child of God you really have something! You have eternal life. Thank you, Jesus, for your gift of salvation.

And fell down on his face at his feet, giving him thanks: and he was a Samaritan. Luke 17:16

When was the last time you fell at the feet of Jesus and thanked Him for what He's done for you? Should you do it now? Take time to thank the Lord for His goodness.

And Jesus answering said, Were there not ten cleansed? but where are the nine? Luke 17:17

Nine out of ten lepers forgot to thank Jesus for their miracle of healing. Let's not be guilty of the same spirit of ingratitude. Thank the Lord for what He's done in your life.

Then believed they his words; they sang his praise. Psalm 106:12

What a great order of service for worship. Let's believe His Word and sing His praises. What an uplift this will be to troubled hearts.

O praise the LORD, all ye nations: praise him, all ye people. For his merciful kindness is great toward us:

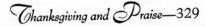

*and the truth of the LORD endureth for ever. Praise
ye the LORD. Psalm 117:1-2*

Take time to praise the Lord! He is worthy of all our
praise and more.

*O give thanks unto the LORD; for he is good: for his
mercy endureth for ever. Psalm 136:1*

Take time to thank the Lord. He is so merciful toward
us. God is so good.

*And to stand every morning to thank and praise the
LORD, and likewise at even. 1 Chronicles 23:30*

This is the kind of exercise that we all need. It keeps
the soul in good shape.

*Oh that men would praise the LORD for his goodness,
and for his wonderful works to the children of men!
Psalm 107:8*

If we did more praising and less complaining we would be much happier.

Blessed be the Lord, who daily loadeth us with benefits, even the God of our salvation. Selah.
Psalm 68:19

The Lord provides for His own. Be sure to thank Him for His daily blessings.

But he that glorieth, let him glory in the Lord.
2 Corinthians 10:17

The Lord deserves all the glory and credit. Praise Him with your words and your actions.

This is the day which the LORD hath made; we will rejoice and be glad in it. Psalm 118:24

Every day is a gift from God. Be glad in the Lord and live it to the fullest.

I am the LORD: that is my name: and my glory will I not give to another, neither my praise to graven images. Isaiah 42:8

The Lord will not share His glory with another. Be sure to Give Him the praise that He deserves. We serve a great and mightly God.

No man taketh it from me, but I lay it down of myself. I have power to lay it down, and I have power to take it again. This commandment have I received of my Father. John 10:18

Jesus voluntarily laid down His life for us so that we might have abundant life and life eternal. Thank you, Jesus.

And Jesus answering said, Were there not ten cleansed? but where are the nine? There are not found that returned to give glory to God, save this stranger. Luke 17:17-18

Take time to express your thanks to the Lord. It will honor God and bless your life too.

He hath not dealt with us after our sins; nor rewarded us according to our iniquities.
Psalm 103:10

Thank God for His mercy! Where would we be without Him?

Rejoice evermore. Pray without ceasing. In every thing give thanks: for this is the will of God in Christ Jesus concerning you. 1 Thessalonians 5:16-18

This is the way to live. Let joy, prayer and thanksgiving be a part of your life.

Enter into his gates with thanksgiving, and into his courts with praise: be thankful unto him, and bless his name. For the LORD is good; his mercy is everlasting; and his truth endureth to all generations. Psalm 100:5

The Lord is worthy of all praise and thanksgiving. Take time to show the Lord that you love and appreciate him.

Think About It

If a man say, I love God, and hateth his brother, he is a liar: for he that loveth not his brother whom he hath seen, how can he love God whom he hath not seen? 1 John 4:20

It's a good question. If you have hate in your heart, something is wrong. Ask God to take the bitterness out of your heart.

But Daniel purposed in his heart that he would not defile himself with the portion of the king's meat, nor with the wine which he drank: therefore he requested of the prince of the eunuchs that he might not defile himself. Daniel 1:8

Have we purposed in our hearts not to defile ourselves with things that do not please God? Let's be holy people for the glory of God.

The proverbs of Solomon. A wise son maketh a glad father: but a foolish son is the heaviness of his mother. Proverbs 10:1

Are you a source of joy or sadness? Follow the Lord's way and you will be a blessing to those around you.

Enlarge the place of thy tent, and let them stretch forth the curtains of thine habitations: spare not, lengthen thy cords, and strengthen thy stakes. Isaiah 54:2

There are times we must expand our spiritual horizons. Are you growing in the Lord? Trust God and move forward with Him.

Let the words of my mouth, and the meditation of my heart, be acceptable in thy sight, O LORD, my strength, and my redeemer. Psalm 19:14

Have you stopped to reflect upon your life like the psalmist did his? It may be time for a good spiritual checkup.

Walk in wisdom toward them that are without,
redeeming the time. Colossians 4:5

Are you making the most of your time and opportunity?
Remember, everyday is a gift from God.

He that refuseth instruction despiseth his own soul:
but he that heareth reproof getteth understanding.
Proverbs 15:32

Are you teachable or stubborn? Let the Lord teach
you and you will gain wisdom and understanding.

God hath spoken once; twice have I heard this; that
power belongeth unto God. Psalm 62:11

Do you face the impossible? Turn to the One who has
all the power you need and more.

For it is better, if the will of God be so, that ye suffer
for well doing, than for evil doing. 1 Peter 3:17

If we're suffering, are we suffering for the right reasons? Let's do God's will no matter what may come.

In whom the god of this world hath blinded the minds of them which believe not, lest the light of the glorious gospel of Christ, who is the image of God, should shine unto them. 2 Corinthians 4:4

It is no accident that people who reject Jesus believe as they do. They are blinded by the Devil. Could that be you?

And God blessed them, and God said unto them, Be fruitful, and multiply, and replenish the earth, and subdue it: and have dominion over the fish of the sea, and over the fowl of the air, and over every living thing that moveth upon the earth.
Genesis 1:28

A materialistic society turns the table on the Word of God. Materialism means that things have dominion over men. God's order means that man has rule over things. Do you own your things or do your things own you?

For he took away the altars of the strange gods, and the high places, and brake down the images, and cut down the groves: And commanded Judah to seek the LORD God of their fathers, and to do the law and the commandment. 2 Chronicles 14:3-4

Are we allowing altars to strange gods to be built in our lives? Take them away. Love and serve the Lord with all your heart.

For he was a good man, and full of the Holy Ghost and of faith: and much people was added unto the Lord. Acts 11:24

Are we a positive influence for the glory of God? We need to be in this day and time. Honor the Lord with your attitude and actions.

Then said Jesus unto his disciples, If any man will come after me, let him deny himself, and take up his cross, and follow me. Matthew 16:24

Are you Jesus' disciple? The job description has just been quoted. The benefits are incredible. Follow the Lord.

And he reared up the court round about the
tabernacle and the altar, and set up the hanging of
the court gate. So Moses finished the work.
Exodus 40:33

Is your life filled with unfinished promises and projects for God? Follow Moses' example. Complete what you have begun.

And Joshua said unto the people, Sanctify
yourselves: for to morrow the LORD will
do wonders among you. Joshua 3:5

We need to be prepared for God and His work. Are you ready? Set your heart upon the Lord.

As yet I am as strong this day as I was in the day
that Moses sent me: as my strength was then, even so
is my strength now, for war, both to go out, and to
come in. Joshua 14:11

Caleb found out that serving the Lord brings strength and vitality to life. Is your life unproductive? Serve the Lord and see how He will make life worth living.

Be not thou afraid when one is made rich, when the glory of his house is increased; For when he dieth he shall carry nothing away: his glory shall not descend after him. Psalm 49:16-17

How much will we leave materially when we die? The answer is simple. We will leave it all. Invest your life in things eternal.

For he hath made him to be sin for us, who knew no sin; that we might be made the righteousness of God in him. 2 Corinthians 5:21

Don't forget the price that Jesus paid for you. What have you done for Him lately?

While we look not at the things which are seen, but at the things which are not seen: for the things which are seen are temporal; but the things which are not seen are eternal. 2 Corinthians 4:18

Have you checked your spiritual eyesight lately? Make sure you have your eyes and heart on things that really matter.

Even so every good tree bringeth forth good fruit;
but a corrupt tree bringeth forth evil fruit. . .
Wherefore by their fruits ye shall know them.
Matthew 7:17, 20

What kind of fruit are our lives producing?

Therefore whosoever heareth these sayings of mine,
and doeth them, I will liken him unto a wise man,
which built his house upon a rock. Matthew 7:24

A wise man not only hears the Word of God but also
practices what he hears. How wise are you?

So teach us to number our days, that we may apply
our hearts unto wisdom. Psalm 90:12

This life won't last forever. Are you making the most
of it?

I beseech you therefore, brethren, by the mercies of
God, that ye present your bodies a living sacrifice,

342— *Think About It*

holy, acceptable unto God, which is your reasonable service. And be not conformed to this world: but be ye transformed by the renewing of your mind, that ye may prove what is that good, and acceptable, and perfect, will of God. Romans 12:1-2

We have too many conformed church people and not near enough transformed people. Which one are you?

Keep thy foot when thou goest to the house of God, and be more ready to hear, than to give the sacrifice of fools: for they consider not that they do evil. Ecclesiates 5:1

Do you listen when you go to the house of the Lord? Come to God with a hungry and eager heart and He will fill your cup.

And the world passeth away, and the lust thereof: but he that doeth the will of God abideth for ever. 1 John 2:17

We can invest our lives in the things of this world that pass away or we can invest our lives in the Lord and His work which lasts forever. Which one will you choose?

Thus saith the L<small>ORD</small>, What iniquity have your fathers found in me, that they are gone far from me, and have walked after vanity, and are become vain?
Jeremiah 2:5

What a penetrating question for God's people? How could we ever be complacent or even rebellious about the Lord who gave His all for us?

Except the L<small>ORD</small> build the house, they labour in vain that build it: except the L<small>ORD</small> keep the city, the watchman waketh but in vain. It is vain for you to rise up early, to sit up late, to eat the bread of sorrows: for so he giveth his beloved sleep.
Psalm 127:1-2

Only what's done in the name of the Lord will stand the test of time and eternity. Is your life counting for the important things in life?

Thirty and two years old was he when he began to reign, and he reigned in Jerusalem eight years, and departed without being desired. Howbeit they buried him in the city of David, but not in the sepulchres of the kings. 2 Chronicles 21:20

What a sad commentary on anyone's life. When we die will we be missed? Let's love the Lord and others while we have the opportunity.

But the fruit of the Spirit is love, joy, peace, longsuffering, gentleness, goodness, faith, Meekness, temperance: against such there is no law.
Galatians 5:22-23

This is a spiritual check list that tells us if we are really filled with the Holy Spirit. How are you doing?

And I, brethren, could not speak unto you as unto spiritual, but as unto carnal, even as unto babes in Christ. I have fed you with milk, and not with meat: for hitherto ye were not able to bear it, neither yet now are ye able. 1 Corinthians 3:1-2

Christian, are you still a baby in the Word when you should be growing into full maturity? "But grow in grace, and in the knowledge of our Lord and Savior Jesus Christ. To him be glory both now and for ever. Amen" (2 Peter 3:18). Get going and growing for the Lord.

Whether therefore ye eat, or drink, or whatsoever ye do, do all to the glory of God. 1 Corinthians 10:31

This gets Christianity down to the basics. How are we doing?

Nevertheless I have somewhat against thee, because thou hast left thy first love. Revelation 2:4

Christian, have you stopped loving the Lord as you should? Remember what He did for you on the cross.

For none of us liveth to himself, and no man dieth to himself. Romans 14:7

You do influence others. Is it for good or evil? Think it over.

I will take no bullock out of thy house, nor he goats out of thy folds. For every beast of the forest is mine, and the cattle upon a thousand hills. I know all the fowls of the mountains: and the wild beasts of the

field are mine. If I were hungry, I would not tell thee:
for the world is mine, and the fulness thereof.
Psalm 50:9-12

This is just a reminder to let us know that this is God's world.

The sacrifices of God are a broken spirit: a broken
and a contrite heart, O God, thou wilt not despise.
Psalm 51:17

God doesn't just want an external show of religion. He wants people who are deeply devoted to Him. Which kind of person are you?

If he set his heart upon man, if he gather unto
himself his spirit and his breath; All flesh shall
perish together, and man shall turn again unto dust.
Job 34:14-15

As you busy yourself with daily activities, pause to remember that you are alive by the sustaining grace of God. Don't forget the Lord.

Ye blind guides, which strain at a gnat, and swallow a camel. Matthew 23:24

Are we sometimes guilty of straining gnats and swallowing camels? Let's allow the Lord to get our priorities in order.

Professing themselves to be wise, they became fools. Romans 1:22

Look around you. How many people fall into this category. We will never know real wisdom until we trust the Lord. "The fear of the Lord is the beginning of wisdom."

Why do the heathen rage, and the people imagine a vain thing? The kings of the earth set themselves, and the rulers take counsel together, against the LORD, and against his anointed. Psalm 2:1-2

Rulers and nations that rebel against the Lord will be as the heathen who rage. Perhaps this is why our civilization looks so uncivilized. Think it over.

For my people have committed two evils; they have forsaken me the fountain of living waters, and hewed them out cisterns, broken cisterns, that can hold no water. Jeremiah 2:13

How can people who know the Lord who gives abundant life follow the world's ways that don't satisfy? It's a mystery.

I will behave myself wisely in a perfect way. O when wilt thou come unto me? I will walk within my house with a perfect heart. Psalm 101:2

Being a godly person in our home should be our first priority. Walk within your home with a perfect heart.

Now therefore thus saith the LORD of hosts; Consider your ways. Haggai 1:5

Who are you? Where are you going? What are the goals of your life? Is your life honoring the Lord? Take time to reflect over these very important questions.

*And when he was come near, he beheld the city, and
wept over it, Luke 19:41*

I wonder how many cities Jesus weeps over today. Is
He weeping over yours? Live a life pleasing to God
and make a difference in your city.

*For laying aside the commandment of God, ye hold
the tradition of men, as the washing of pots and
cups: and many other such like things ye do.
Mark 7:8*

Traditions are no substitute for obedience to God and
love for God.

*Love not the world, neither the things that are in the
world. If any man love the world, the love of the
Father is not in him. 1 John 2:15*

The Christian is to love the Lord more than the things
of the world. What is your first love?

*For where your treasure is, there will your heart
be also. Luke 12:34*

What do you really treasure? Do you treasure a relationship with Jesus? This is our greatest treasure.

*Righteousness exalteth a nation: but sin is a
reproach to any people. Proverbs 14:34*

Under which category would God place our nation?

Inspirational Library

Beautiful purse/pocket size editions of Christian classics bound in flexible leatherette. These books make thoughtful gifts for everyone on your list, including yourself!

The Bible Promise Book   Over 1000 promises from God's Word arranged by topic. What does God promise about matters like: Anger, Illness, Jealousy, Love, Money, Old Age, and Mercy? Find out in this book!
Flexible Leatherette $3.97

Daily Light   One of the most popular daily devotionals with readings for both morning and evening.
Flexible Leatherette $4.97

Wisdom from the Bible   Daily thoughts from Proverbs which communicate truths about ourselves and the world around us.
Flexible Leatherette $4.97

My Daily Prayer Journal   Each page is dated and features a Scripture verse and ample room for you to record your thoughts, prayers, and praises. One page for each day of the year.
Flexible Leatherette $4.97

Available wherever books are sold.
Or order from:

Barbour Publishing, Inc.
P.O. Box 719
Uhrichsville, OH 44683
http://www.barbourbooks.com

If you order by mail add $2.00 to your order for shipping.
Prices subject to change without notice.